I0102721

○ human rights *first*

Baseless Prosecutions of Human Rights Defenders in Colombia
In the Dock and Under the Gun

February 2009

About Human Rights First

Human Rights First believes that building respect for human rights and the rule of law will help ensure the dignity to which every individual is entitled and will stem tyranny, extremism, intolerance, and violence.

Human Rights First protects people at risk: refugees who flee persecution, victims of crimes against humanity or other mass human rights violations, victims of discrimination, those whose rights are eroded in the name of national security, and human rights advocates who are targeted for defending the rights of others. These groups are often the first victims of societal instability and breakdown; their treatment is a harbinger of wider-scale repression. Human Rights First works to prevent violations against these groups and to seek justice and accountability for violations against them.

Human Rights First is practical and effective. We advocate for change at the highest levels of national and international policymaking. We seek justice through the courts. We raise awareness and understanding through the media. We build coalitions among those with divergent views. And we mobilize people to act.

Human Rights First is a nonprofit, nonpartisan international human rights organization based in New York and Washington D.C. To maintain our independence, we accept no government funding.

This report is available for free online at www.humanrightsfirst.org

© 2009 Human Rights First. All Rights Reserved.

Acknowledgements

Written by Andrew Hudson, Senior Associate, Human Rights Defenders Program.

Andrew Ehrinpreis, Laura Rogers, and Martha Bucaram provided invaluable research assistance. Mike McClintock, Matt Easton, and Gabor Rona provided editorial comments and Sarah Graham designed the book. Thanks to all the Colombian human rights defenders who spent considerable time finding the court documents needed to compile this report.

Cover Photos

Colombian human rights defenders [from left to right]: Iván Cepeda, Martín Sandoval, Fanny Perdomo, Alfredo Molano, Principe Gabriel González, Fr. Javier Giraldo, Nieves Mayuza, Alfredo Correa de Andreis, Héctor Hugo Torres, Gustavo Gallon, Carmelo Agamez, Julio Avella, Carmen Mayuza, Teófilo Acuña, Andrés Gil, Francisco Ramírez, Amaury Padilla, José Humberto Torres, Berenice Celeyta, José Murillo Tobo.

{ } human rights *first*

Headquarters

333 Seventh Avenue
13th Floor
New York, NY 10001-5108

Tel.: 212.845.5200
Fax: 212.845.5299

Washington D.C. Office

100 Maryland Avenue, NE
Suite 500
Washington, DC 20002-5625

Tel: 202.547.5692
Fax: 202.543.5999

www.humanrightsfirst.org

Table of Contents

List of Acronyms and Institutions

Colombian State

CEAT (*Cuerpo Élite Antiterrorista*): Elite Anti-Terrorist Unit of the National Police.

DAS (*Departamento Administrativo de Seguridad*): Administrative Security Department. The national intelligence service.

GAULA (*Grupo de Acción Unificada por la Libertad Personal*): Group of Unified Action for Personal Liberty. Elite units from the armed forces tasked with combating kidnappings.

Judicial Inspector (*Procurador Judicial*): Part of the Office of Inspector General responsible for monitoring criminal investigations.

Judicial Police (*Policia Judicial*): Agents from the various institutions below that carry out investigation and intelligence activities at the instruction of the Office of the Prosecutor General.

- SIJIN (*Seccional Judicial de Inteligencia*): Judicial and Investigative Police. The National Police's division of intelligence and investigation.

- DIJIN (*Dirección De Investigación Criminal*): Direction of Criminal Investigation. The National Police's criminal investigation division.

- CTI (*Cuerpo Técnico de Investigación*): Technical Investigation Unit. The Prosecutor General's unit responsible for investigation and forensic assistance in criminal cases.

- DAS: See above.

Office of the Inspector General (*Procuraduría General de la Nación*): State institution that conducts disciplinary investigations of public officials and monitors state actions.

Office of the Ombudsman (*Defensoria del Pueblo de Colombia*): State entity charged with promoting and upholding human rights.

Office of the Prosecutor General (*Fiscalia General de la Nación*): State entity that is formally independent of the Executive and responsible for most criminal investigations and prosecutions.

RIME (*Regional de Inteligencia Militar del Ejército*): Regional Military Intelligence Unit of the National Army.

Others

AUC (*Auto Defensas Unidas de Colombia*): United Self-Defense Forces of Colombia, the largest coalition of paramilitary groups.

ELN (*Ejército de Liberación Nacional de Colombia*): National Liberation Army, a smaller insurgent guerrilla group.

FARC (*Fuerzas Armadas Revolucionarias de Colombia*): Revolutionary Armed Forces of Colombia, the largest guerrilla group in Colombia.

IACHR: Inter-American Commission on Human Rights, an autonomous organ of the Organization of American States (OAS) with a mandate to promote and protect human rights in the Americas. The IACHR can grant precautionary measures, which a state should implement to protect the human rights of individuals.

Caribbean
Sea

PANAMA

Pacific
Ocean

VENEZUELA

Riohacha

Santa Marta
Barranquilla
ATLANTICO
Cartagena

LA GUAJIRA

MAGDALENA

Valledupar

CESAR

Sincelejo
SUCRE
Monteria
CORDOBA
BOLIVAR

NORTE
DE
SANTANDER

Cucuta

Rio Magdalena

Rio Cauca

Rio Atrato

ANTIOQUIA

Bucaramanga
SANTANDER

Arauca

ARAUCA

Rio Meta

Puerto Carreno

CHOCO

Medellin

Rio Magdalena

BOYACA
Tunja

CASANARE

Quibdo

CALDAS
RISARALDA   Manizales
SAN ANDRES
Y PROVIDENCIA   Pereira
Armenia
QUINDIO   Ibaque

CUNDNAMARCA

Yopal

VICHADA

Rio Cauca

Bogota

Villavicencio

DISTRITO
CAPITAL

Rio Meta

Puerto
Inirida

VALLE DEL CAUCA

Cali

TOLIMA

META

COLOMBIA

GUAINIA

Rio Guaviare

Rio Guainia

Neiva
CAUCA   HUILA
Popayan

San Jose del
Guaviare

NARINO

Florencia

GUAVIARE

Rio Vaupes

Mitu

Pasto   Mocoa

CAQUETA

VAUPES

ECUADOR

PUTUMAYO

AMAZONAS

Rio Caqueta

BRAZIL

Rio Putumayo

Rio Ica

PERU

Amazon

Leticia

Colombia

- - · - ·   International Boundary
- - · · -   Parish Boundary
★   National Capital
◉   Parish Capital
·········   Railroad
———   Road

0   100   200 Kilometers
0   100   200 Miles

Executive Summary

"If they cannot assassinate you, they follow you, threaten you and prosecute you. They prosecute us for whatever matter."

Francisco Ramirez, human rights lawyer and president of the Colombian Mine Workers' Union SINTRAMINERCOL[1]

"Belonging to an organization that defends human rights... carries with it a high risk: constant stigmatization by the media and people who occupy public positions.... [T]hey may try to assemble false criminal charges against people who work in these organizations... which means that judicial institutions must be cautious in the analysis of each element of the evidence."

Hernando Betancur, 3rd Prosecutor, Medellín[2]

Francisco Ramirez, Colombian human rights lawyer

IN A CRIMINAL JUSTICE SYSTEM plagued by impunity, the tenacity with which Colombian prosecutors pursue human rights defenders for supposed crimes is striking. While corruption and arbitrary actions are a systemic problem throughout the judicial system, those who peacefully promote human rights are singled out for particular intimidation through baseless investigations and prosecutions. Unfounded charges are often widely publicized, undermining the credibility of defenders and marking them as targets for physical attack, often by paramilitary groups.

While defenders are not alone in being subjected to false investigations, their persecution is distinctive due to the nature of the charges and the methods of collecting, and falsifying, evidence. They are usually accused of rebellion and membership in a guerrilla organization. By the time defenders are illegally detained, they have often been investigated in secret for many months or even years. Two of the hallmarks distinctive to defenders' cases are the use of false testimony from ex-combatants and of inadmissible intelligence files. Charges are typically based on spurious allegations by ex-guerrillas whose testimony has been coerced or coached by regional prosecutors. Armed with such erroneous evidence, which is objectively inadequate to initiate an investigation, prosecutors and others publicly pre-judge the defendants, stigmatizing defenders as terrorists. Because defenders are singled out for this type of persecution, solutions that focus specifically on defenders are needed.

The steadfast investigation of spurious criminal complaints against defenders stands in stark contrast to the failure to investigate attacks, threats, and other forms of intimidation perpetrated against them or against civilians more generally. The Colombian state also fails to prosecute or otherwise discipline judicial officials who instigate such specious prosecutions.

Human rights defenders in Colombia play a legitimate and essential role in protecting basic rights and strengthening democratic institutions. Charges against them are often politically motivated and intended primarily to discredit and stigmatize them individually and as a class. Unfounded criminal charges are damaging in many ways:

- The stigmatization of defenders as terrorist sympathizers places them at considerable risk of reprisal and death threats by paramilitaries or others;

- The proceedings force defenders to expend time and resources defending themselves, diminishing their capacity to perform productive human rights work;

- The charges discredit defenders and tarnish their reputations as legitimate human rights activists; and

- The threat of political prosecution has a chilling effect, encouraging defenders to practice self-censorship and limit their activities. In relation to Colombia, the U.N. Special Representative on Human Rights Defenders has stated that such "proceedings are part of a strategy to silence human rights defenders."[3]

Despite increasing attention to the issue, in the absence of a detailed study, some Colombian officials refuse to acknowledge that there is a widespread problem. Human Rights First has spent more than a year researching and documenting 32 cases of unfounded prosecutions against defenders. Analysis of primary materials such as interviews with defenders, defense briefs, prosecutors' resolutions, and judicial sentences reveal the spurious nature of these criminal investigations. For the first time, this report reveals a positive development: prosecutors and judges all over Colombia are recognizing the existence of malicious prosecutions against defenders. However, it is not enough to identify the problem or to mitigate its effects after damage has been done. There must be fundamental changes in the justice system.

As a major supporter of judicial reform in Colombia, the United States can play a constructive role in combating malicious prosecutions of human rights defenders. It is clearly in the interests of the United States to have a vibrant civil society in Colombia, which can freely express ideas and strengthen respect for the rule of law.

Based on an analysis of 32 cases and extensive interviews with government officials and human rights defenders, Human Rights First makes the following recommendations.

Recommendations

To the Colombian Authorities:

1. The Prosecutor General, or the prosecutors in charge of each case, should close the unfounded criminal investigations against the human rights defenders identified in this report.

2. The Prosecutor General should pass a resolution empowering his Human Rights Unit in Bogotá to coordinate the review of all criminal investigations against human rights defenders. Its role should be similar to that which it currently assumes in relation to investigations of enforced disappearances.[4] That Unit should be able to quickly vet the investigation for compliance with due process standards or rapidly delegate the review to the regional prosecutorial Human Rights Unit, if appropriate. All cases found to be specious should be closed immediately. Human rights defenders should be able to lodge complaints directly with the unit. In deciding which cases to review, the Unit should adopt the broad definition of human rights defenders used by the U.N.

3. The Prosecutor General should conduct a comprehensive internal investigation into corruption and connections between justice officials and paramilitaries or successor groups, focusing on regional prosecutors. The state should dismiss from judicial and prosecutorial institutions all individuals shown to be corrupt or connected to illegal armed groups.

4. The Prosecutor General should discipline and prosecute all prosecutors found to have breached the law in falsely investigating human rights defenders.

5. Prosecutors should reject patently implausible witness testimony, refrain from influencing witness testimony, and carefully evaluate witness testimony from ex-combatants who are receiving reintegration benefits. Prosecutors should also provide the accused with any evidence that may impeach the witness's credibility.

6. The Prosecutor General should issue a resolution or directive addressed to all judicial and prosecutorial institutions reemphasizing relevant international law (cited in this report) and provisions of the new Colombian Procedural Code. Those laws set standards for impartial investigations and fair trials and bar politically motivated criminal proceedings against human rights defenders and others.

7. All public officials should refrain from making statements that discredit or stigmatize human rights defenders as guerrillas. The President should enact a new Presidential Directive to this effect, similar to those issued by previous administrations.

8. The Inspector General's office should ensure that its judicial inspectors promptly and consistently intervene in cases of malicious prosecutions of human rights defenders. Judicial inspectors should support the dismissal of specious charges against defenders.

9. The Colombian Congress should amend the *Intelligence and Counter-Intelligence Bill* before it to better regulate the collection and use of information in government intelligence reports. The Inspector General should be empowered to review, in an unannounced manner, intelligence reports from any state institution to exclude from those reports all manifestly unfounded information that incriminates or is prejudicial to individuals, including human rights defenders. The law should clarify that information may not be collected for arbitrary reasons, such as membership in a human rights organization, and should also include a bar on the dissemination of information from intelligence reports.

10. Congress should amend the Colombian Criminal Code to decriminalize the offenses of slander and libel. While legitimate as civil complaints, such criminal offenses are incompatible with the protection of human rights.

To the Government of the United States:

11. The U.S. government at the highest level should publicly support Colombian human rights defenders and this message should not be undercut by subsequent statements or policies.

12. U.S. government officials should continue to raise individual cases of specious prosecutions of human rights defenders with their Colombian counterparts and emphasize that such persecution breaches the U.S. Guiding Principles on Non-Government Organizations. In addition, at the highest political levels, U.S. foreign policy should respond to the denigration of human rights defenders by Colombian public officials.

13. The U.S. government should support and assist in implementing the structural reforms and recommendations contained in this report, to address the problem at a systemic level. For example:

    • The U.S. Agency for International Development (USAID), a major source of funding for judicial reform in Colombia, should work with the Prosecutor General and the Ombudsman to implement an education program for prosecutors and judges concerning the value of human rights advocacy. The program should emphasize that human rights advocacy has no connection with terrorism and is protected by Colombian and international law.

    • USAID and the U.S. Department of Justice should support the Prosecutor General to enable the Human Rights Unit to monitor and review all criminal investigations against human rights defenders as envisioned in the second recommendation above. Such support could include funding, technical assistance, and training.

14. The U.S. Congress should include in appropriations legislation a condition requiring certification by the State Department that the Colombian armed forces are not involved in human rights violations against human rights defenders.

15. In certifying foreign assistance to Colombia under current appropriations legislation, the Department of State should consider the role the armed forces play in assisting malicious prosecutions of defenders.

16. The Department of State should end the practice of denying or revoking visas to Colombian human rights defenders based on the fact that they have been subject to a specious criminal prosecution or unfairly branded as a terrorist by public officials.

To the Inter-American Commission on Human Rights:

17. The Commission should hold a hearing in March 2009 on allegations of malicious prosecutions of human rights defenders in Colombia. It should also support implementation of this report's recommendations by including them in its 2009 follow-up report on the situation of human rights defenders in the region.

Introduction

"We know they manufacture accusations [against defenders]"

> Colombian Deputy Prosecutor General Guillermo Mendoza[5]

"While the actions of human rights defenders are founded in constructing an authentic rule of law, malicious prosecutions, among other forms of persecution, represent a degeneration of that law. The state trivializes justice and criminalizes collective conscience."

> Danilo Rueda, Director, Inter-Church Commission for Justice and Peace[6]

INTERNAL ARMED CONFLICT has existed in Colombia since at least the 1960s, when the Revolutionary Armed Forces of Colombia (*Fuerzas Armadas Revolucionarias de Colombia, or* FARC) and later the National Liberation Army (Ejército de Liberación Nacional de Colombia, or ELN) began engaging in guerrilla insurgency against the Colombian state. Paramilitary groups were initially formed to support the government and fight the insurgents. Decades of conflict has displaced millions of civilians, while both guerillas and paramilitaries have increasingly played a role in drug trafficking and organized crime. Paramilitaries, originally under the direction of regular armed forces, have now supposedly demobilized. Various legal frameworks have allowed members of illegal armed groups to obtain legal, economic, protective, health, and educational benefits if they demobilized and cooperated with authorities (see section II. A.). Paramilitary structures clearly remain intact, however, as evidenced by their continual threats and attacks against civilians and human rights defenders.[7]

One legacy of the conflict and the political polarization it produced is that Colombia is one of the most dangerous states in the world for human rights defenders. A human rights defender is anyone who nonviolently promotes or protects human rights.[8] In Colombia, authorities and paramilitaries have traditionally assumed that defenders are leftists, and thus sympathetic to the guerrilla movement, and have subjected them to considerable persecution. Dozens of human rights defenders are murdered every year, including labor rights activists, lawyers, indigenous leaders, members of non-governmental organizations (NGOs), and community and religious leaders. Reports estimate that from 2002 to 2006, 138 human rights defenders were killed or disappeared.[9] Defenders also face a range of other attacks and forms of intimidation, such as smear campaigns and break-ins, threatening and omnipresent surveillance, death threats, physical assaults, kidnapping, violence directed toward family members, and assassination attempts. In very few cases are those responsible brought to justice.

Behind these high levels of violence and intimidation lie two related and pernicious types of attacks against Colombian defenders: stigmatization as terrorist sympathizers and unfounded criminal prosecutions.[10] This report focuses on the latter problem, the use of politically motivated criminal charges to harass,

---

Overview of a Typical Specious Investigation of a Defender

False criminal investigations of human rights defenders follow a clear pattern. A regional prosecutor generally initiates a preliminary investigation of a defender in secret. During that stage the prosecutor may receive intelligence reports from the army, judicial police, or other state security entities, usually containing irrelevant and inflammatory material. The prosecutor obtains false, incoherent, or contradictory witness testimony from ex-combatants receiving reintegration benefits from the state. At this stage of evidence-gathering, the defender is likely arrested and detained and subsequently, often significantly later, charged with rebellion for allegedly being a terrorist or guerilla. Under section 467 of the Criminal Code, rebellion is defined as any "attempt to destroy the national government or abolish or amend the constitutional regime by employing arms..."[11] In none of the cases reviewed in this report was there any evidence of a defender resorting to the use of violence or arms. Instead, the prosecution usually relies on innuendo and the assertion that the defender is covertly involved with the FARC.

The investigation is often closed by a senior prosecutor after the defense has sought a review of the case. This report refers to such individuals as reviewing prosecutors. There is no automatic review process, however; the defense must use a variety of legal motions to appeal an initial prosecutor's decision in order to seek a review from another prosecutor or judge. An investigation may be closed after only a few days, though in some cases the investigation, and detention, can extend for years. Occasionally the prosecutor proceeds to trial, where the judge is likely to acquit the defender. However, in a small number of cases defenders have been found guilty of rebellion, even though the evidence objectively did not support such a verdict. Even if the investigation is promptly closed, as the example of Alfredo Andreis de Correa illustrates (see Case 12, Annex), the defender remains stigmatized as a terrorist and at considerable risk of attack. Many defenders are systematically harassed by paramilitaries after an investigation is closed, sometimes forcing them to leave the country.

---

stigmatize, detain, and endanger the lives of human rights defenders. These criminal charges typically:

- are based on two unreliable sources: false allegations by ex-combatants receiving economic benefits from the state and intelligence reports that contain false information;

- entail prolonged arbitrary detention, sometimes for years, during open-ended criminal investigations; and

- pertain to offenses that are particularly open to politically-motivated misuse, including rebellion, slander, and defamation.

Criminal investigations of human rights defenders take place in a broader context marked by human rights violations in the name of combating terrorism and defending "democratic security." Colombia is one of many states that, since 2001, have enacted counterterrorism laws, policies, and practices that are used to suppress the legitimate conduct of human rights defenders and marginalized groups.[12] Under this rubric, detention of members of other groups is also common in Colombia. For example, in November 2008, a prosecutor ordered the disproportionate inspection of all databases and books of five universities from 1992-2008 to find evidence of students and teachers connected to subversive groups, leading to a number of arrests.[13] The same prosecutor also ordered the interception of emails and telephone conversations of over 150 people, including many human rights defenders.[14] Corruption and failure to abide by national and international due process standards are endemic to the criminal justice system in Colombia.

Alfredo Correa de Andreis
Murdered after Stigmatization by
Malicious Prosecution

Alfredo Correa de Andreis was a well known soci-
ologist, human rights activist, and professor at the
University of Magdalena. The Administrative Security Department (DAS) detained him in Barranquilla
on June 17, 2004, and the 33rd Prosecutor of
Cartagena soon accused him of rebellion and of
membership in the the FARC. He was subsequently
released after a judge found the case against him
to be baseless. However, on September 17, shortly
after his release, he was killed by presumed paramilitaries who apparently believed the prosecutor's
assertion. In April 2006, a former senior ranking
official of the DAS reported that the agency had
provided paramilitaries with a "death list" on which
Correa allegedly appeared.[15]

between defenders on paramilitary "hit lists" and those
subject to specious prosecution. This combination of
intimidation intensifies the legal, financial, and
psychological impact on defenders.

One positive trend is that some Colombian prosecutors
and judges are effectively reviewing cases and
dismissing specious prosecutions when they can.
Frequently these prosecutors are from regional Human
Rights Units, which are well versed in due process
standards. The case may come before them because
the defense has appealed a decision by the initial
prosecutor, such as the imposition of preventative
detention. However, even if a prosecutor reviews and
closes the investigation, the damage is done. Widely
publicized accusations undermine the credibility of
defenders and mark them as targets of physical attack.
Long after investigations have closed, defenders
continue to receive death threats. The Correa case, at
left, demonstrates that even if the judicial system
resolves baseless prosecutions, defenders remain at
risk. The Colombian government must therefore ensure
not just that malicious prosecutions are closed, but that
they are not initiated in the first place.

Some aspects of the Colombian state provide important
support to human rights defenders. Frequently,
defenders receive official protection from the Justice
and Interior Ministry in recognition of their dangerous
profession. The protection program provides physical
protective measures such as phones, bodyguards, and
even bulletproof cars, to a wide variety of human rights
defenders and to representatives of other vulnerable
groups such as Afro-Colombians.[16] The inter-agency
program considers the risk that a particular individual
faces and what degree of protection is warranted.

Nevertheless, this report demonstrates clear patterns
and practices that set the judicial mistreatment of
defenders apart from that of the general population.

Spurious investigations can also have particularly severe
consequences for defenders beyond the judicial system.
For example, prosecutions are frequently accompanied
by death threats from paramilitaries or harassment from
the armed forces. There is also considerable overlap

Taped Telephone Conversation Reveals Practice of Bringing Trumped-Up Charges

Father Javier Giraldo

On October 7, 2008, Colombian media outlets reported on a phone conversation between retired General Rito Alejo Del Río and former Justice and Interior Minister Fernando Londoño Hoyos. The two men are heard planning to lodge false criminal complaints against the Inter-Church Justice and Peace Commission (CIJP) and one of its founders, Father Javier Giraldo.[17] CIJP is an internationally renowned human rights organization that peacefully protects and upholds the rights of marginalized communities such as Afro-Colombians and indigenous people.[18] For many years Fr. Giraldo and CIJP have condemned human rights violations allegedly committed by General Del Río as commander of the army's 17th Brigade in Urabá, Antioquia, from 1995 to 1997. Del Río is currently incarcerated, charged with complicity in the 1997 paramilitary murder of rural leader Marino López. CIJP represents López in these criminal proceedings.

In the taped conversation, Del Río and Hoyos discuss how to discredit CIJP. Hoyos conjectures that by instructing others to publicly denounce CIJP, "it will allow us to criminally condemn the priest." Del Río responds, "Yes, of course, of course." Del Río also indicates that he has previously tried to encourage false criminal investigations against defenders. The phone conversation reveals that a former army general and justice minister think it is acceptable to intimidate and discredit activists who seek to expose human rights violations. The conversation also shows the connection between public stigmatization and criminal prosecution, in this case indicating that public accusations make it easier to file charges.

The existence of this program raises the question of why other institutions, usually regional prosecutors, maliciously prosecute defenders as terrorists. One explanation for this inconsistency is that the Colombian state is not a unitary actor and, despite the existence of institutions to protect human rights defenders, many public officials do not show them same respect. A defender, especially in remote regions and conflict areas, may challenge corrupt prosecutors or illegal armed groups that pressure those prosecutors. A false prosecution is one way to attempt to deter defenders from their human rights advocacy.

The problem, however, is by no means just at the local level. While there is no evidence of a central policy of the President or Prosecutor General to maliciously prosecute defenders, senior government officials from the national intelligence service, the army, and the Interior and Justice Ministry have directly conducted specious criminal investigations. Senior officials also routinely encourage the perception that defenders are terrorists. From the head of state down, these officials have denied the legitimacy of human rights work, encouraging the false belief that human rights advocacy is intrinsically linked to subversive activity.

The central government also bears responsibility for failure to correct a systemic problem. Prosecutors and others who engage in false prosecutions of human rights defenders are seldom reprimanded or investigated, implying that the state condones such actions.

Such a widespread problem requires a vigorous response from all components of the Colombian state. The recent establishment of a new Criminal Procedural

Code is a welcome development in promoting impartial prosecutions (see Section II for more details). However, the new code requires better implementation, as malicious prosecutions of defenders continue.

The use of baseless charges against Colombian human rights defenders has been recognized by the United Nations, the inter-American system for human rights, the United States government, and even members of the Colombian government.[19] Following the publication of a White Paper in 2007 on malicious prosecutions,[20] Human Rights First provided further focus on the issue, advocating on behalf of Colombian human rights defenders subjected to spurious criminal charges.[21] In a trip to Colombia in late 2007, Human Rights First met with senior members of the Colombian government and policymakers from various state institutions to discuss the problem.[22]

Despite this attention, in the absence of a study devoted exclusively to the phenomenon, some Colombian officials continue to express doubt that the problem is prevalent.[23] Human Rights First has spent more than a year researching and documenting 32 individual cases of unfounded prosecutions against defenders in the last four years (see Annex). Analysis of primary materials in these cases, such as defense briefs, prosecutors' resolutions, and judicial sentences, reveals the spurious nature of the criminal investigations. The list of cases in this report is not exhaustive, as verifying the cases and obtaining the necessary documents proved impossible in some instances, and some cases may not have come to the attention of Human Rights First at all. However, the cases included in this report allow for the distillation and analysis of common themes in order to expose the root causes of the problem and identify policy prescriptions.

The report consists of seven chapters that describe key aspects of the problem with case examples interwoven into each chapter. The report also contains a series of recommendations to combat the problem and an Annex containing a summary of 32 emblematic cases.

I. Colombian and International Legal Standards on Due Process

INTERNATIONAL LAW obligates Colombia to provide all defendants with fair trials and investigations that abide by due process, including the right to cross examine witnesses, to be informed promptly of all charges, and to be afforded the presumption of innocence.[24] Colombia has ratified both the International Covenant on Civil and Political Rights (ICCPR) and the American Convention on Human Rights (ACHR), which protect many rights violated by the spurious criminal investigation of a human rights defender.[25] The right to a fair trial is contained in the ICCPR (article 14), the ACHR (article 8), the Basic Principles on the Role of Lawyers,[26] and the Basic Principles for the Treatment of Prisoners.[27] Under the old Procedural Code, witnesses frequently did not attend a trial, leaving the defense unable to examine them. This is a clear breach of article 14(3)(e) of the ICCPR and article 8(2)(f) of the ACHR. The right of a defendant to be informed promptly of the nature and cause of the charges against them is enshrined in article 14(3)(a) of the ICCPR and is frequently breached when human rights defenders are detained for long periods without charge. By publishing photos and identifying defenders as guerrilla fighters before trial, prosecutors fundamentally undermine the presumption of innocence recognized by article 14(2) of the ICCPR and article 8(2) of the ACHR. The right to liberty is also protected by article 9 of the ICCPR and article 7 of the ACHR. Those articles are breached when defenders are not informed of the reasons for their arrest or are not brought promptly before a judge, or where a court does not determine the lawfulness of that detention.

International law also prescribes standards of due process that a prosecutor should uphold. Article 14 of the U.N. Guidelines on the Role of Prosecutors states that "prosecutors shall not initiate or continue prosecution, or shall make every effort to stay proceedings, when an impartial investigation shows the charge to be unfounded." [28]

Freedom of expression is a fundamental right also accorded protection in the ICCPR and ACHR and many other international legal documents.[29] The United Nations Human Rights Defenders Declaration, which celebrated its 10th anniversary in 2008, specifically recognizes the right that everyone has to "discuss, form and hold opinions on the observance ... of all human rights ... and, through these and other appropriate means, to draw public attention to these matters..."[30]

Colombian criminal law is also quite detailed about the level of evidence needed by a prosecutor to initiate an investigation. Article 397 of the Criminal Procedural Code states, "The prosecutor... will formally charge the accused only when the occurrence of an act can be demonstrated and a confession or testimony exists which shows serious and credible motive, serious evidence and is supported by documents, or other probative means which indicate the responsibility of the defendant."[31] Finally, article 234 directs officials such as prosecutors to "search and determine the real truth. They must ascertain with equal zeal both the circumstances that demonstrate the existence of the punishable conduct as well as those that reduce or

Criminal Procedure in Colombia

Until recently, Colombia had a standard inquisitorial or civil law criminal justice system, which differs significantly to common law systems such as that in the United States.[32] Under the inquisitorial criminal system, fact-finding is done by an investigative prosecutor who plays the role of an inquisitor with the objective of ascertaining the truth. The prosecutor has broad powers to compel testimony and collect evidence. The prosecutor must seek out both exculpatory and incriminating evidence in order to assess whether there is sufficient evidence for trial. All evidence collected, and testimony taken, is compiled in a file and submitted to the judges appointed to the case. During the investigative phase, the accused has the right to be present while the investigative prosecutor collects evidence.

Colombia has recently shifted from an inquisitorial to an accusatory criminal justice system. Law 906 of 2004 established a new Criminal Procedural Code, which progressively took effect in different regions of Colombia from 2005 to 2008.[33] The new Code provides stronger protections and stricter guarantees of due process than the Procedural Code that applied before.[34] For example, the new Code requires that witnesses be present at trial to be cross-examined by the defense. Given that many of the cases in this report were prosecuted under the old Code, the provisions from that Code are cited in this report. Although very recent and new cases will be subject to the new Code, these changes alone will not solve the problem of malicious prosecutions of human rights defenders. Many of the criminal investigations of human rights defenders were filed under, and continue to be governed by, the old Code. Moreover, recent illegal detentions in the Sandoval and Agamez cases demonstrate that the new Code is not being implemented in practice (see Cases 29 and 2, Annex).

exonerate the responsibility of the accused or that demonstrate their innocence."[35]

President Álvaro Uribe has also committed his government to due process standards by recognizing the U.S. State Department Guiding Principles on Non-Governmental Organizations ("Guiding Principles"). On April 30, 2007, President Uribe said that the Colombian government was "preaching and practicing" the values contained in the Guiding Principles. [36] Principle 5 of the Guiding Principles states, "Criminal and civil legal actions brought by governments against NGOs, like those brought against all individuals and organizations, should be based on tenets of due process and equality before the law." [37] A number of executive directives issued prior to the administration of President Uribe enshrine similar protections for human rights defenders and direct Colombian public officials to abstain from making false accusations against defenders.[38]

Other more specific Colombian criminal law protections are mentioned in different chapters of this report.

II. Problems with Witness Testimony

CRIMINAL INVESTIGATIONS against defenders often rely on testimony from ex-combatants or guerrilla informants with close relationships to government authorities. These witnesses have deserted the FARC or other groups and sought benefits that encourage members of armed groups to demobilize and reintegrate into society.[39] Of the 28 relevant cases listed in the Annex, at least 17 rely on reintegrated witnesses. The remaining four slander cases are not relevant to this section of the report. The inherently unreliable nature of such evidence is compounded by indications that the testimony is coached or otherwise influenced by public officials. Much of the testimony that results is vague, incoherent, and contradictory.

A. Unreliable Nature of Witnesses Receiving Reintegration Benefits

Evidence from witnesses receiving reintegration benefits must be treated with particular care. While such testimony can provide valuable information about guerrilla activities, it can also incriminate innocent people.[40] The Colombian legal framework for reintegration allows members of illegal armed groups to obtain legal, economic, protective, health, and educational benefits if they demobilize and cooperate with authorities. Demobilized individuals can in fact receive amnesties for certain crimes.[41] Colombian superior court jurisprudence, including from the Constitutional Court, states that the testimony from such witnesses must be treated suspiciously because it comes from witnesses who are not impartial and who benefit by collaborating with authorities.[42] One judge concluded, "For such testimonies to be credible they must be analyzed and evaluated with particular rigor and care, because a superficial examination could give rise to the commission of grave injustices."[43] However, in investigations of defenders, such witness testimony is frequently neither properly evaluated nor corroborated, and many regional prosecutors assume that it is reliable and credible.

B. Manipulation of Witness Testimony

"The armed forces suspect someone has links with the guerrillas, then look for any help to support this, and then suddenly an informant appears who is compensated."

> Deputy Prosecutor General Guillermo Mendoza[44]

In addition to using inherently unreliable witnesses, prosecutors, the armed forces or DAS frequently interfere with their testimony. Prosecutors have apparently coached or led witnesses by directly instructing them what should appear in their declarations. For example:

■ In the ACVC case (see Case 2, Annex), the reviewing Human Rights Unit prosecutor stated, "The testimonies collected may appear similar but taken holistically they are not credible and show signs of having been coached so as to discredit ACVC."[45]

Unreliable and Partial Witnesses: Alejandro Quiceno and Elkin de Jesús Ramirez

Alejandro Quiceno (pictured) is a young human rights activist who works for various human rights organizations in Medellin (see Case 28, Annex). The 5ᵗ Specialized Prosecutor in Medellin detained him on March 30, 2005, and charged him with rebellion. In September 2005, Prosecutor 153 of Medellin found the detention unjustified and ordered his release. She stated that the testimonies of the reintegrated witnesses involved were unreliable since they were only seeking benefits from the government: "They search for benefits from the state and society and in order to obtain them, many times they do not consider the real consequences of their testimony, harming innocent people who have nothing to do with the situation."[46]

Elkin de Jesús Ramirez is a human rights lawyer with the Legal Liberty Organization (*Corporacion Juridica Libertad*) in Medellin. In November 2006 he was charged with rebellion by Prosecutor 74 in Antioquia, accused of military, political, and ideological indoctrination of seditious groups. After more than a year, in January 2008 a reviewing prosecutor in Antioquia dismissed the case finding that the witness testimony provided by reintegrated witnesses was incoherent, illogical, unreasonable, and contradictory.[47] Specifically, the prosecutor stated that the reintegrated witnesses may have given biased testimonies in order to obtain economic benefits established under government reintegration programs: "This is what happens with the statements of those who various years after laying down weapons, suddenly appear before authorities ...to relate facts that could have been denounced earlier but that is done at that moment, without doubt, to obtain the benefits established by [the government's reintegration benefit program]."[48]

■ A human rights lawyer with the Young Persons Network in Medellin, Claudia Montoya represents young people illegally detained and physically abused by public authorities. On October 18, 2006, members of the Prosecutor General's Technical Investigation Unit (CTI) and police arrested Montoya. Prosecutor 57 in Medellin charged her with rebellion. After months in prison and under house arrest, in February 2007 a reviewing prosecutor closed the investigation. She found that witness statements were worded almost identically, so as to suggest interference and coaching by the initial prosecutor.[49] Another reviewing prosecutor found that the witnesses were led by the initial prosecutor who told the witnesses they should identify Montoya as the accused before any of them had mentioned her name (see Case 23, Annex).[50]

Prosecutors have also shown photos of human rights defenders to witnesses and even provided the name of the defender in question (see, for example, Cases 11, 23, and 24, Annex). Such practices undermine due process and render flawed any subsequent positive identification of the defender as the perpetrator. In many of the resolutions and judgments analyzed by Human Rights First, reviewing prosecutors and judges quoted sections from different witness statements that were identically worded, indicating coaching from the initial prosecutor. For example, in dismissing rebellion charges against Amaury Padilla (see Case 24, Annex), the Prosecutor General found that the written testimonies of two witnesses were not credible owing to the fact that they were essentially identical and appeared copied.[51] He also stated that one witness had access to other witness declarations and that DAS had suggested to witnesses that Padilla was the perpetrator, and he surmised that there was "manipulation in certain facets" of the investigation against Padilla.[52] The Prosecutor

---

Judicial System is Used to Target Human Rights Defenders: Príncipe Gabriel González

Príncipe Gabriel González Arango is a prominent student leader in Santander department.[53] On January 4, 2006, he was detained in Bucaramanga and falsely accused of rebellion and of leading an urban militia force. At the time he was Regional Coordinator of the Political Prisoners Solidarity Committee (*Fundacion Comité de Solidaridad con los Presos Políticos*, or CSPP). After fifteen months, he was released from prison after a judge in Bucaramanga acquitted him of all charges. The judge recognized that the legal system was being manipulated and dismissed witness evidence in part "due to the fear that evidence was being used to direct the judicial system against those who are fighting for social or democratic causes or claiming their rights."[54] The only other witness in the case told the CSPP that her witness statements were made under duress from members of the police and the CTI in Bucaramanga.[55] Despite being released, González continues to receive death threats and appears on public paramilitary "death lists."

General also concluded, "These testimonies have so many defects a rational investigation of criminal responsibility is not possible and the elements of knowledge and evidence as required by the law are not present."[56] Padilla works for one of Colombia's leading human rights organizations, the Association for Alternative Social Promotion (MINGA) in Bogotá. By the time charges were dropped, Padilla had spent more than five months in detention.

Some judges have even recognized the use by prosecutors of "professional witnesses" to make false declarations against defenders. For example, in December 2007 Hector Hugo Torres was detained by the Judicial and Investigative Police (SIJIN) in Bosa, Bogotá, accused of rebellion (see Case 32, Annex).[57] Torres is President of the Human Rights and International Humanitarian Law Commission in Bajo Ariari. Two days after his detention, a judge ordered his immediate release. The judge found that Torres's defense and due process rights had been violated and that the prosecution had failed to observe basic rules of procedure. She stated, "The Prosecutor General has used 'professional witnesses' in different judicial processes to accuse farmers, community leaders and possibly other social leaders. These witnesses live in military installations and receive economic and legal benefits to make false declarations against innocent people—these witnesses are the proof presented against Hector Torres..."[58]

C. Inconsistent, Contradictory, and Vague Witness Testimony

Another hallmark of witness testimony in criminal investigations of defenders is its inconsistent, contradictory, and vague nature. Of the 28 relevant cases in the Annex, at least 16 involve incoherent or implausible witness testimony that does not meet basic evidentiary standards. Frequently witnesses are unable to accurately describe, identify, or name the human rights defender as the supposed guerrilla leader they are

Witnesses Coached by Prosecutor and Armed Forces: José Murillo Tobo

On August 21, 2003, authorities in Arauca detained 18 civil society leaders, including labor and community organizers such as José Vicente Murillo Tobo (President of the Joel Sierra Human Rights Committee) and Alonso Campiño Bedoya (Director of the Central Workers Union in Arauca). Both Murillo and Campiño had previously been granted protective measures by the Inter-American Commission on Human Rights (IACHR). After almost six months of detention, Murillo and Campiño were charged with rebellion.[59] Three years later, Murillo, Campiño and 16 others were found guilty of rebellion by the Criminal Court of Saravena Circuit in Bogotá. The decision was appealed and is now pending before the Superior Tribunal of Arauca. Murillo and others were released given that their 37 months in pre-trial detention exceeded the sentence handed down.

The prosecutor that initiated the investigation has its headquarters within the 18th Brigade of the National Army. Two key witnesses were reintegrated guerrillas who negotiated guarantees for immunity from prosecution in January 2003. According to the defense, they spent seven months in the headquarters of the 18· Brigade immediately before charges were brought against the defendants. The defense maintains that during this time the prosecutor and army coached them to denounce Murillo, possibly in retaliation for his work exposing alleged human rights violations by the 18· Brigade.[60] Some other witnesses in the case admitted that their evidence had been prepared by the prosecutor and army.[61]

impeaching. Reviewing prosecutors or judges often dismiss criminal investigations against defenders because they find the witness testimony contradictory or inconsistent. In comments that are applicable to many such cases, one judge characterized witness allegations as "mere speculation that aimed to distort,"[62] concluding that their "assertions could not be supported in light of the rules governing evaluation of evidence, because of their internal contradictions and... far-fetched nature."[63] In other cases against defenders, prosecutors trained in human rights have found the witness testimony to be vague, reliant on hearsay information, and consisting of no more than conjecture and suspicions (for example, see the ACVC case below).

However, in spite of significant contradictions between witnesses, initiating prosecutors rarely attempt to corroborate the veracity of witness testimony. In closing the investigation into Elkin Ramirez (see Case 27, Annex), a reviewing prosecutor found the testimonies incoherent, contradictory, and illogical. For example,

one witness wrote that Ramirez frequently visited a FARC camp alone, while another witness said Ramirez barely ever visited and did so with others.[64] Another witness claimed that he did not see Ramirez after 2002, but later stated that he saw Ramirez in 2003. Still another witness said that he saw Ramirez in the town of Argelia in 2002, when the prosecution knew that the witness was not in Argelia in 2002. The reviewing prosecutor concluded that the "credibility or morality of a witness suffers when their assertions harbor incoherencies which cannot be explained by result to logic, experience or reasonableness. In this situation their assertions are not admissible." [65]

Vague and Implausible Witness Testimony: The Rural Association of Rio Cimitarra Valley

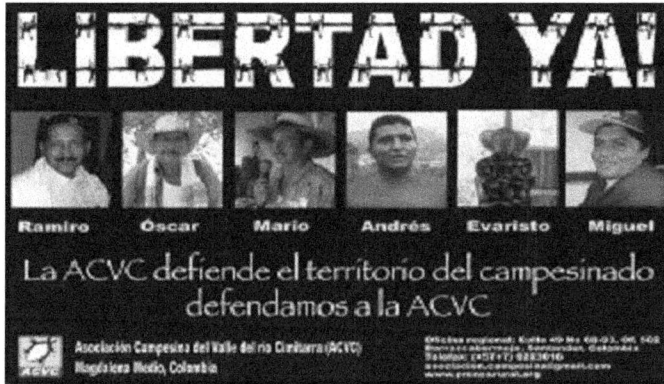

The Rural Association of Rio Cimitarra Valley (*Asociacion Campesina del Valle del Rio Cimitarra*, or ACVC) combines human rights advocacy with mobilization around rural socio-economic issues, such as land rights and development. The IACHR recognized the legitimacy of its members' work and the risks they face by awarding them precautionary measures in 1999 and 2000.[66] On September 29, 2007, the majority of ACVC's board of directors, including Oscar Duque, Mario Martinez, Evaristo Mena, and Andres Gil, were arrested and charged with rebellion.[67] With the arrest of two other leaders, Miguel Gonzalez and Ramiro Ortega, in January 2008, ACVC's entire board of directors was in prison or under investigation.[68] In April and May 2008, the charges against all but Gonzalez and Gil were dismissed by a reviewing prosecutor from the regional Human Rights Unit.[69] In dismissing the charges, the reviewing prosecutor stated that the prosecution's witnesses lacked specificity regarding which criminal activities were supposedly committed and that their testimony was not corroborated by supporting evidence. He found that their testimony was "no more than personal opinion and should have been verified forcefully by the investigative agencies."[70] Although their cases are based on the same testimony, Gonzalez and Gil remain in prison and are currently facing trial.

In reviewing the case of Amaury Padilla (see Case 24, Annex), the Prosecutor General found that the testimonies of witnesses were so riddled with inconsistencies and contradictions as to require dismissal of the charges for lack of serious evidence. He stated, "The intrinsic and extrinsic contradictions in the witnesses' statements go against the rules of experience and, furthermore... from all this it can be inferred that there was manipulation in certain facets."[71] For example, of the five different witnesses (four of whom were ex-guerrillas receiving reintegration benefits), none provided the same alias to identify Padilla as an alleged FARC member. Other inconsistencies included the supposed role that Padilla played in the FARC. Some alleged he had a military role and was seen in FARC camps for extended periods and participated in kidnappings. Other witnesses stated that his role was purely political and ideological. Furthermore, the Prosecutor General could not understand how the original prosecutor could have found either of these contradictory allegations persuasive since Padilla would have been noticeably absent from his high-profile job working for the Governor of Bolivar Department in Cartagena.[72] An objective initiating prosecutor reviewing both the testimony used to incriminate Padilla and publicly available records would have concluded that a criminal investigation was baseless.

III. Illegal Reliance on False and Unreliable Intelligence Reports

"Witnesses who testify on the basis of intelligence files are not real witnesses, they are cloned witnesses"

> Gustavo Gallon, Colombian Commission of Jurists[73]

A. Use of Inadmissible Intelligence Reports

Compounding the use of coached and unreliable witnesses, prosecutors often turn to a second source of flawed evidence when charging human rights defenders: uncorroborated intelligence files or reports. Of the 28 relevant cases that Human Rights First has analyzed in the Annex, at least 14 involve reliance on flawed intelligence reports. These reports are usually prepared by the armed forces or by one of the various institutions that make up the judicial police (see list of acronyms). Prosecutors regularly rely solely on these intelligence reports to initiate and continue a criminal investigation against a defender.

Colombian law clearly prohibits this practice. Under both the old and new Criminal Procedural Code, intelligence reports are not admissible evidence nor do they have independent probative value. Article 314 of the old code states that reports by the judicial police do not have "the value of testimony or evidence and can only serve as criterion to guide the investigation." A 1999 law further amended the Procedural Code to be

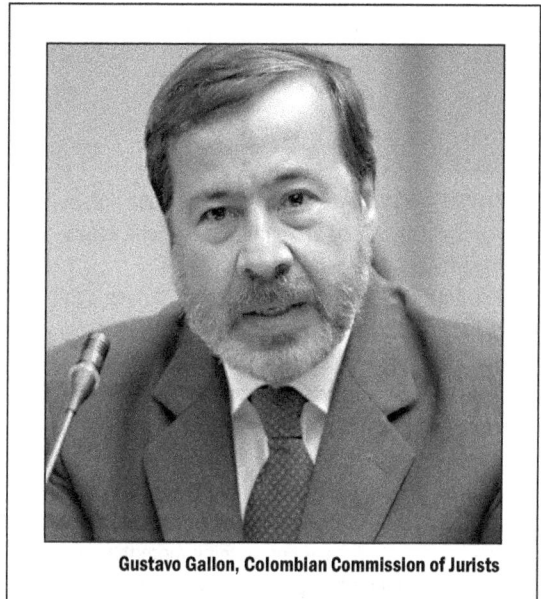

Gustavo Gallon, Colombian Commission of Jurists

explicit on this point: "In no case will the report of the Judicial Police and the testimonies provided by informants have probative value in the prosecution."[74] In interpreting the Procedural Code, the Constitutional Court has clarified that:

- no intelligence report or testimony provided by reintegrated witnesses can be used as evidence;[75]

- information can only be gathered by intelligence agencies where reasonable evidence exists to suggest that the relevant individual may have acted illegally;[76]

Army Intelligence Reports Used as a Basis for Prosecution: Teofilo Acuña

Teofilo Acuña is President of the Federation of Agro-Mining Unions in South Bolivar (*Federación Agrominera del Sur de Bolivar* or FEDEAGROMISBOL). He has exposed human rights violations committed by the New Granada Military Battalion and represents communities in South Bolivar opposed to extraction of resources by multinational mining companies. Following his arrest on April 26, 2007, in Santa Rosa, South Bolivar, the 28ᵗ Prosecutor in Simiti, Cartagena, accused him of rebellion. The prosecutor initiated the investigation based on nothing more than an intelligence report prepared by the New Granada Military Battalion, a unit that killed Acuña's predecessor at FEDEAGROMISBOL, and that had been the target of Acuña's human rights advocacy.[77] The Battalion was also responsible for the reportedly violent arrest of Acuña and has a history of serious human rights violations.[78] After ten days of detention, the same prosecutor released him by way of a resolution admitting insufficient evidence and noting that intelligence reports have no probative value according to Colombian law.[79] However, Acuña's safety is now at greater risk, and the Colombian government has stated that the investigation against Acuña remains open.[80]

- information in intelligence reports must not be divulged to third parties;[81] and

- if appropriate precautions are not taken, intelligence reports become "an accumulation of dangerous affirmations without any probative substance."[82]

Numerous prosecutors have also recognized this legal restriction. In 1994 one prosecutor stated, "From the strictly legal point of view it is not admissible to assimilate intelligence reports into criminal investigations or to take them as evidence."[83] In dismissing the ACVC case in 2008, the prosecutor stated clearly, "Mere statements by the investigative officials can not be given probative value unto themselves without proper corroboration."[84]

B. Unreliability of Intelligence Reports

Intelligence reports are not legally admissible for good reason. They often contain information that is fallacious and inflammatory and they rarely provide hard proof of a defender's involvement with guerilla groups, instead containing general statements of opinion and conflating human rights advocacy with terrorism. In the case of Principe Gabriel Gonzalez (see Case 17, Annex), for instance, the intelligence report only referred to a supposed guerilla by an alias, with no indication that the alias belonged to Gonzalez. Nevertheless, the prosecutor used the intelligence report to incriminate Gonzalez.[85]

Intelligence reports usually constitute no more than a summary of dubious witness statements without any new, independent evidence to corroborate those statements. As the legal process moves forward, prosecutors compound the problem by encouraging witness statements that repeat the speculation contained in the reports, as noted above.

Operation Dragon

Operation Dragon was a covert information-gathering exercise and apparent plot to assassinate human rights defenders, union leaders, and members of the political opposition in Colombia.[86] In August 2004, a CTI review uncovered a series of official documents that reportedly detailed the following aspects of Operation Dragon:

Berenice Celeyta

- The Department of Military Intelligence in the third Brigade of the Colombian Army in Cali was paying two private security companies to gather information on 170 human rights defenders and politicians in Cali. Those people include well-known human rights activist Berenice Celeyta, President of the Association for Investigation and Social Action (NOMADESC), and Senator Alexander Lopez, now President of the Senate's Human Rights Commission.

- The surveillance and information gathering was intended to be used in a plan to execute some of these people, including Senator Lopez.

- The third Brigade, the CTI unit in Cali, Cali police, and the DAS allegedly supported and collaborated in gathering intelligence about the human rights defenders.

- One secret military intelligence report falsely stated that a number of the human rights defenders were engaged in terrorism and subversive activities.[87]

- An official memo from the Prosecutor General's office falsely identified Celeyta, Senator Lopez, and 11 other human rights defenders as being part of a terrorist network with links to the Irish Republican Army (IRA), FARC, and ELN.[88]

Operation Dragon is a clear example of public officials from the Colombian Army, police, Prosecutor General's office, and DAS fabricating information about human rights defenders in intelligence reports in order to detain them, initiate specious criminal charges against them, or endanger their lives. After more than three years and a court order, the Prosecutor General officially opened a preliminary investigation into Operation Dragon. As of January 2009 no one has been prosecuted.[89]

Human rights organizations in Colombia suggest that military officials, armed with false intelligence reports that incriminate human rights defenders, pressure prosecutors to initiate investigations.[90] For example, Victor Julio Laguado Boada is an agrarian social leader in Arauca working with the agricultural cooperative COAGROSARARE. On October 24, 2006, a prosecutor in Arauca opened an investigation into Laguado for rebellion and issued an arrest warrant (see Case 19, Annex).[91] According to the defense, the investigation was started by a prosecutor based at the headquarters of the army's 18th Brigade on the basis of two intelligence reports prepared by the police and the army.[92] These close ties limit not only the prosecutor's independence but also the possibility of access by victims and witnesses to make statements and testify free from pressure, fear, or additional risk.[93] The subsequent witness testimony collected by two reintegrated guerrillas was inconsistent and contradictory and did nothing more than reiterate the contents of the intelligence reports.

Uncorroborated intelligence files are not only used to initiate investigations but are also provided to the media. For example, on September 1, 2008, a television news outlet published a government intelligence report stating that NGOs such as the Association for the Promotion of Social Alternatives (MINGA) "had been responsible for helping members of the FARC and ELN emigrate to Canada."[94] In response to a letter from Human Rights First about this incident, the Defense Ministry claimed that there were no intelligence reports that contained information on human rights defenders, an assertion contradicted by many of the cases cited in this report.[95] Dissemination of false information about MINGA to the mass media endangers the lives of those that work for the organization and raises the specter that they may be subject to future specious criminal proceedings based on this intelligence report.

IV. Prosecutorial Bias

"The government promotes a sinister connection between social organizations and subversion."

> José Humberto Torres, human rights lawyer, Committee for Solidarity with Political Prisoners[96]

Prosecutors are to "search and determine the real truth. They must ascertain with equal zeal both the circumstances that demonstrate the existence of the punishable conduct as well as those that reduce or exonerate the responsibility of the accused or that demonstrate their innocence."

> Article 234 of the old Procedural Criminal Code[97]

UNDER COLOMBIAN and international law, prosecutors should not continue proceedings when an impartial investigation would show the charge to be unfounded. These standards are already violated by the use of unreliable and uncorroborated evidence described above. However, some prosecutors demonstrate additional prejudice toward a predetermined outcome by beginning an investigation or filing charges in the absence of any evidence at all, or without considering the exculpatory evidence as required by law. The widespread and dangerous practice of publicly describing defenders as terrorists before a trial has even begun further highlights the tendency to conclude guilt prematurely.

A. Insufficient Proof to Justify Investigation and Failure to Consider Exculpatory Evidence

It is frequently difficult to understand on what basis a prosecutor has initiated an investigation against a human rights defender. In dismissing the charges against Claudia Montoya, a reviewing prosecutor stated, "Naturally this investigation lacked relevant diligence. The CTI said that certain information was obtained from interviews by prosecution witnesses, but the truth is that studied thoroughly these testimonies do not provide such information."[98] See case 23, Annex for further details.

In many cases, at the time of a defender's arrest, the witnesses have not identified or named him or her. Their testimony is often so incoherent, far-fetched, and self-contradictory that it fails to reach even the most rudimentary standard of evidence required to underpin the serious charges. Any impartial investigation would reveal the charges, and the evidence upon which they relied, to be unfounded. However, prosecutors frequently do not investigate exculpatory evidence that would conclusively prove the defender's innocence. In these circumstances, the fact that investigations continue appears to demonstrate a lack of objectivity.

Defenders Detained for Years Based on "Mere Suspicions": Mayuza Sisters

Nieves Mayuza is an activist in the National Federation of Agricultural Farming Unions (*Federación Nacional Sindical Unitaria Agropecuaria*, or FENSUAGRO). Her sister Carmen Mayuza is a regional leader with the Colombian health workers' trade union (ANTHOC). Carmen led a campaign to stop the privatization of hospitals and to defend free access to healthcare and workers' rights. Both were arrested on May 11, 2006, with Fanny Perdomo Hite (see below and Case 26, Annex), and all were charged with rebellion for alleged involvement in kidnappings by the 53· Front of the FARC. They were detained for over two years before they were found not guilty. In her decision, Judge Carmen Arrieta from the Bogota Criminal Circuit Court 53 held that the investigation was too subjective and ignored clear exculpatory evidence, such as testimony from members of the 53· Front of the FARC who testified they had never seen the Mayuza sisters.[99] A judicial inspector reviewing the case from the Inspector General's office found that the minimum substantial requirements to accuse the sisters had not been met.[100] Moreover he stated that in order to charge them with rebellion, it was necessary to gather actual indications of responsibility for a crime rather than "mere suspicions."[101]

Nieves Mayuza (above),
Carmen Mayuz (below)

Defender Detained for Two Years for Providing Sister with Gifts: Fanny Perdomo

Fanny Perdomo Hite was a member of Citizens Community for Life and Peace (*La Comunidad Civil de Vida y Paz*, or CIVIPAZ), an organization of displaced citizens working peacefully to reclaim appropriated land. Her brother, Reinaldo Perdomo, was murdered by suspected paramilitaries in August 2003, presumably because of his human rights advocacy. Fanny Perdomo was arrested on May 11, 2006, on suspicion of kidnapping and rebellion. The kidnapping charges were quickly dropped and she was tried for rebellion by the 9· Prosecutor in the Anti-Kidnapping and Extortion Unit in Bogotá. After over two years of detention, she was acquitted in June 2008.[102] The only evidence the prosecutor had linking Perdomo with the FARC was her purchase of hair and feminine hygiene products and a telephone card for her sister, who the prosecutor alleged was a FARC member. The judge rightly stated that Perdomo's provision of a phone card and hygiene products to her sister for personal use was not a criminal activity and could in no way support a claim that Perdomo engaged in rebellion. The judge stated "the ties of kinship that exist among sisters allow them to engage in gestures of generosity, even if one of them is acting outside the law."[103] If the prosecutor had followed appropriate laws and standards, it is unlikely he or she would have concluded that Perdomo had committed rebellion by giving her sister these gifts.

Furthermore, the proactive nature of investigations against defenders stands in stark contrast to the lack of investigation or prosecution for many serious crimes in Colombia.[104] The Colombian justice system suffers from corruption, and a lack of resources and expertise. Many serious crimes, and especially crimes committed against human rights defenders, remain unpunished.[105] Given such widespread impunity, the decision to prosecute cases against defenders on the basis of patently unreliable evidence demonstrates prosecutors' disregard for their function and the rule of law.

For example, in the case of Amaury Padilla (cited above and in Case 24, Annex), the Prosecutor General dismissed the case, citing the alarming lack of preparation by the prosecutor who opened the investigation against Padilla. Neither DAS nor the prosecutor could apparently say which officials interrogated one of the witnesses. Moreover, the Prosecutor General noted that the initial prosecutor did not even interrogate that witness, but rather relied on a transcript provided by DAS.[106] These insights into the prosecution generate grave doubts about the process through which that witness was deposed or even why he was deposed. It is also unclear how, given the scant and faulty evidence, the investigating prosecutor could reasonably order Padilla detained for six months.

B. Publicly Equating Human Rights Defenders with Terrorists

"The stigmatization against human rights defenders originates fundamentally from the government, headed by President Uribe, his presidential adviser José Obdulio Gaviria, and other sectors of the extreme right. They have been generating a climate of polarization, hostility and false evidence, the conse-quences of which are detentions of human rights defenders."

> Luis Jairo Ramirez, Executive Director, Permanent Committee for Human Rights[107]

DAS, the army, and regional prosecutors have consis-tently shown a propensity to detain human rights defenders and publicly smear them as terrorists, often before formal charges have been brought. Such behavior renders a fair trial impossible and breaches the presumption of innocence by which all prosecutors and judicial authorities must abide. Moreover, in a politically polarized society such as Colombia, this stigmatization puts the lives of defenders at grave risk by potentially encouraging attacks against defenders. By publicly marking the individual as a FARC terrorist, such allegations encourage attacks against the defender by paramilitaries or others (see, for example, Case 12, Annex). Of the 28 relevant cases listed in the Annex, at least eight involve public pre-trial comments made by state officials equating the defender with terrorism, including the following:

- During the investigation of Juan Carlos Celis Gonzalez, an NGO activist from Bogotá, the prose-cutor reportedly made statements equating Celis' human rights activities with support for the FARC, saying that those activities constituted "instruction, indoctrination, international relations, recruitment, publicity, planning, and infiltration" on behalf of the FARC.[108] Celis was detained for almost a year before the 13th Specialist Prosecutor in Bogotá charged him with rebellion and other related offenses (see Case 10, Annex).[109]

■ Luz Perly Córdoba Mosquera was President of the Rural Association of Arauca (*Asociacion Campesina de Arauca,* or ACA). Notwithstanding both national and international recognition as an important human rights leader,[110] Córdoba was arrested in Arauca by DAS members on February 18, 2004 (see Case 11, Annex). A DAS document reportedly alleged that the ACA was a political arm of the FARC and that Córdoba's human rights advocacy was a façade for terrorism and rebellion.[111] The prosecutor also reportedly stated that human rights advocacy is a part of the FARC's campaign to smear and discredit the Colombian nation.[112] Such comments demonstrate bias by the prosecutor and DAS against Córdoba in particular and human rights defenders in general. It was not until six months later that a prosecutor brought formal charges of rebellion and narco-trafficking against Córdoba; a judge annulled these charges in March 2005.[113]

In addition to public statements, prosecutors have frequently released photos or videos of human rights defenders to the media. Media coverage of defenders as terrorists severely stigmatizes them. Teresa de Jesús Cedeño Galindez is a criminal defense attorney and former President of the Colombian Permanent Committee of Human Rights (CPDH), one of the oldest human rights organizations in the country.[114] On July 30, 2003, the CTI detained Cedeño and others who worked with her in Arauca.[115] Prosecutor 287 in Bogotá charged her with procedural fraud and bribery, although the fraud charges were quickly dropped (see Case 8, Annex). The CTI and prosecutor provided media outlets with a video

of an unidentifiable woman counting money, which was used to publicly denounce Cedeño. The prosecution did not introduce the video as evidence at the trial, but its dissemination may have been intended to prejudice her trial. On appeal, a court criticized the publication of the video on television: "We question the diffusion of the video by the mass media, which ... certainly should have led to an investigation of those authorities responsible for the custody of this piece of evidence."[116] The publication of the video before trial likely breached articles 7 and 14 of the Colombian Criminal Procedural Code, which respectively protect the presumption of innocence and restrain publicity before trial.

Prosecutors also have a propensity to assert guilt by association. The reviewing prosecutor in the ACVC case noted that just because a person was allegedly seen meeting with an alleged insurgent, does not mean that the person is himself an insurgent (see Case 2, Annex). The prosecutor noted that this is especially important to remember in the Colombian context, where people are often coerced into having contact with guerillas.[117] Prosecutors must have clear evidence to fulfill all the elements of rebellion under article 467 of the Criminal Code, namely an "attempt to destroy the national government" or use of arms to abolish the constitutional regime.[118]

V. Problematic Preliminary Investigation

PROCEDURAL SAFEGUARDS built into Colombian criminal law, such as time limits for investigations and the obligation to inform suspects that they are under investigation, are designed to prevent the use of unreliable evidence and encourage prosecutors to consider evidence impartially. However, prosecutors often ignore these basic safeguards. Under the old Procedural Code, the purpose of a preliminary investigation is for a prosecutor to determine whether illegal conduct has occurred and to obtain evidence in order to identify those responsible for the illegal conduct.[119] Prosecutors frequently detain defenders for longer periods than permitted and conduct investigations without informing the defender of the investigation or even of the subsequent charges. In these circumstances, it appears that preliminary investigations may be used in order to intimidate, silence, or otherwise deter defenders from carrying out their advocacy.

A. Preliminary Investigations Exceed Statutory Time Limits

Article 325 of the Procedural Code states that a preliminary investigation must not exceed six months, yet many human rights defenders have been subject to preliminary investigation for longer periods. A reviewing prosecutor in the case of Alejandro Quiceno found that the initial prosecutor had breached article 325 by engaging in a preliminary investigation for almost a year (see Case 28, Annex).[120] In the case of José Murillo and the Araucan defenders, it appears that the prosecutor engaged in a preliminary investigation for at least eight months, if not longer (see Case 4, Annex).[121] ACVC

alleges that one of its leaders, Andres Gil, was the subject of a preliminary investigation for as long as five years, culminating in his arrest (see Case 2, Annex). [122]

B. Investigations Conducted without Informing the Defendant

Both the Colombian Constitution and the Criminal Procedure Code, as interpreted by the Constitutional Court, make it clear that anyone subject to a preliminary investigation must be notified of its existence by the prosecutor.[123] This requirement derives in part from the presumption of innocence, as well as the right to an effective defense: "The right to be presumed innocent would be violated if the person involved was not informed in a timely manner of the existence of a preliminary investigation against them... they must be informed of the relevant offense as well as be permitted to know the fundamental evidence underpinning the charge."[124] However, when conducting preliminary investigations of human rights defenders, prosecutors rarely inform them of their activities. (For particularly egregious examples, see cases 3, 4, and 26, Annex). Such secret investigations fuel speculation by the human rights community that prosecutors are concocting false charges in collusion with unreliable witnesses.

C. Failure to Promptly Inform Defender of Charges

A related but more serious problem is the failure to inform defendants of the charges against them once the preliminary investigation has been completed and even after they have been arrested. For example, in the case of José Murillo and the other Araucan leaders, it appears a preliminary investigation was opened against them on January 27, 2003, but they were never informed of the investigation. On August 21, 2003, security forces broke into Murillo's house and detained him, allegedly without a warrant. He was held with others for over six months before Special Prosecutor 12 from the National Terrorism Unit finally charged them with rebellion on February 24, 2004 (see Case 4, Annex).[125]

Principe Gabriel Gonzalez was detained for approximately four months before he was informed of the charges against him (see Case 17, Annex), while Cordoba was detained for approximately six months before charges were formalized (see Case 11, Annex). Finally, a judge in Madrid, Cundinamarca, declared the arrest of Aldemar Lozano illegal because he was detained without being informed of the reasons for his arrest or the nature of the charges against him (see Case 20, Annex).[126] Lozano is a community leader for the Inter-Church Justice and Peace Commission (CIJP).

VI. Arbitrary Detention of Human Rights Defenders

Detention is arbitrary "when the deprivation of liberty results from the exercise of fundamental rights or freedoms."

U.N. Working Group on Arbitrary Detention[127]

DEFENDERS ARE FREQUENTLY ARRESTED without a valid warrant, are unjustifiably held in preventative detention, and suffer unacceptable conditions of detention. In fact, human rights defenders were detained in all but one of the relevant cases listed in the Annex. The detention of human rights defenders takes place in the context of the the high level of arbitrary detentions of the general population in Colombia. Coordination Colombia, Europe and United States (CCEEUU), an advocacy and research organization, reported 6,912 arbitrary detentions of civilians between August 2002 and July 2006, with the majority apprehended in groups of ten or more people.[128] While arbitrary detention of anyone is a grave violation of international and Colombian law, the detention of human rights defenders is particularly damaging to the enjoyment of human rights for two reasons. Firstly, it raises the concern that the defender may have been detained as a result of exercising fundamental rights and freedoms, such as the right to freedom of expression and association. Secondly, it has a broader chilling effect on society, sending a clear message that any member of society can also be deprived of his or her liberty. Members of Colombian civil society express concern that the armed forces, DAS, and prosecutors

are acting in a coordinated manner to detain defenders as a form of intimidation.[129]

A. No Valid Warrant for Arrest

There appear to be at least four different ways that defenders are detained without a valid arrest warrant.[130] First, the defenders are arrested with no warrant at all, as in the cases of Juan Carlos Celis Gonzalez and José Murillo Tobo and the other Araucan leaders detained with him (see Cases 8 and 3, Annex). Second, a warrant exists but does not contain information specific enough to allow for the identification of the person to be apprehended. Third, the warrant is filled out during or after the arrest, as was the case with Mauricio José Avilez Alvarez (see Case 6, Annex). Fourth, the arrest warrant is void because it was not executed correctly, as allegedly transpired in the cases of Teofilo Acuña and Elkin Ramirez (see Cases 1 and 26, Annex).

Each of these scenarios breaches both international and Colombian law. In order to issue an arrest warrant, Colombian law requires judicial approval that there is sufficient evidence of punishable conduct; identification of those presumed to have committed the crime; and sufficient motive to presume that those alleged are responsible for crime.[131] Colombian law also states that intelligence reports do not possess independent probative value. However, judicial authorities have frequently awarded arrest warrants solely on the basis of information contained in intelligence reports (see section III above).

Defenders Detained for Exercising Fundamental Rights: Martin Sandoval

On November 4, 2008, a number of human rights leaders in Arauca were detained in an operation that strongly resembled the detention of José Murillo and colleagues in 2003 (see Case 4, Annex).[132] Prosecutor Ruth Tovar Merchan of the 1ᵗ Specialist Prosecutor's Unit in Cucuta and Arauca apparently authorized the detention, accusing the defenders of rebellion.[133] The detentions were carried out by police, DAS, and CTI. Those detained included Martin Sandoval, a well-known human rights activist and the President of the Permanent Committee of Human Rights in Arauca (CPDH Arauca). Sandoval has criticized the government's human rights record in Arauca, especially on such issues as arbitrary detention, forced displacement, and extrajudicial executions.[134] The defenders remain imprisoned and the Prosecutor General has not responded to Human Rights First's request for an explanation for their arrest.

B. Unjustifiable Preventative Detention

The Colombian Procedural Code provides for preventative detention of a person before charges are filed, but the detention is bound by the principle of necessity and proportionality.[135] As such, the prosecutor may impose preventative detention only if:

- there is a demonstrable necessity and the prosecutor has at least two grave and lawfully obtained indications of criminal responsibility, and

- the measures imposed are the least restrictive necessary to ensure the presence of the defendant, the preservation of evidence, and the protection of the community.[136]

However, prosecutors frequently abuse the preventative detention framework to deprive human rights defenders of their liberty without justifying why such detention is necessary or proportionate. In the case of the detention of José Murillo, the prosecutor reportedly never communicated to the defendants why the preventative detention was necessary (see Case 4, Annex).[137] In fact, the defendants were well-known human rights defenders with ongoing ties to the community and were therefore less likely to abscond. In addition, the primary evidence came from witnesses who were quartered in military bases, and were thus in no danger from the defendants. In addition, the Colombian state breaches defenders' rights under article 9(4) of the ICCPR and article 7(6) of the ACHR if defenders are not able to take proceedings to a court to determine the legality of their detention.

In the case involving various ACVC leaders, the defendants were also subject to preventative detention (see Case 2, Annex). After one month, the 3ʳᵈ Prosecutor in Barrancabermeja rejected their motion to annul the detention. In doing so, the prosecutor articulated a troubling standard for the revocation of preventative detention.[138] The prosecutor stated that detention measures can be revoked only where new evidence is presented by the defendants—a standard that would seem to place the burden of proof on defendants rather than on the prosecutor. Adding to this implication was the prosecutor's reference to "provisional liberty" as a "benefit" that the defendants could not enjoy due to the danger they allegedly presented to the community.[139] The arguments presented in favor of preventative detention in this case were similarly troubling. First, the prosecution argued that, because the defendants were charged with a serious crime punishable by up to 13 years in prison, it was not reasonable to expect that they would appear for trial. Second, the prosecution argued that, given the seriousness of the alleged crimes, the defendants represented a danger to the community.[140] The implication of these arguments is that preventative detention measures will be awarded as a matter of course whenever anyone is charged with rebellion. This manipulation of preventative detention clearly contravenes both the Procedural Code and Constitutional Court jurisprudence.

C. Unacceptable Conditions of Detention

It has also been reported that the conditions of detention for human rights defenders are problematic. Defenders have allegedly been abused while in custody,[141] held in disproportionately harsh incarceration,[142] or denied access to a lawyer.[143] In the cases of José Murillo and Claudia Montoya, the defenders were transferred to maximum security prisons and held with convicted criminals in regions of Colombia far from their lawyers, impeding their access to effective defense (see Cases 4 and 23, Annex).

VII. Criminal Defamation and Slander

"Malicious prosecutions against human rights defenders in Colombia has become a perverse practice perpetrated by authorities to block and try to discredit legitimate action."

Agustin Jimenez Cuello, President, Committee for Solidarity with Political Prisoners (CSPP)

IN TYPICAL CASES charging human rights defenders with rebellion, prosecutors fail to satisfy the elements of the crime. With defamation and slander, there is also a faulty legal standard to begin with. These very broad criminal offenses are particularly susceptible to abuse and are frequently used to violate human rights defenders' freedom of expression.

Articles 220–228 of the Colombian Criminal Code create criminal offenses of slander and defamation or libel.[144] Specifically, article 220 states that anyone who "makes dishonorable imputations" about a person commits the criminal offense of slander. Article 221 states that an individual commits criminal defamation when they "falsely attribute criminal conduct to someone." Article 224 creates a defense to these offenses if the statements are proved to be true.

While civil torts of defamation and slander are common around the world, the criminalization of such conduct is problematic. Human rights defenders play a critical role in the formation of public opinion and enhance a society's ability to receive information and divergent ideas. When human rights defenders are prosecuted for their opinions, it deters them from their work and has a wider chilling effect on society, discouraging various forms of political scrutiny and criticism.[145] The IACHR has found that when human rights defenders and others are dissuaded from scrutinizing public officials, "[d]emocracy is transformed into a system in which authoritarianism and human rights violations find fertile ground for imposing themselves..."[146]

Claudia Julieta Duque, a well-known investigative journalist who focuses on human rights issues, was charged with criminal slander and libel following a complaint by Emiro Rojas, a former director of DAS in Antioquia (see Case 13, Annex).[147] Duque had engaged in groundbreaking research into the murder of journalist Jaime Garzon and accused Rojas, head of the DAS, of irregularities in the investigation.[148] Human Rights First is unaware of any action by the prosecutor to investigate the veracity of her claims.

While the criminalization of slander and defamation itself is problematic, prosecutorial practice is also to blame. As the examples of Duque and Cepeda (see box below) demonstrate, criminal slander investigations are usually initiated by prosecutors at the behest of public officials. Prosecutors then rarely explore the veracity of the claims made by human rights defenders, which, if proved true, would absolve them of liability under article 224 of the Criminal Code.

Defender Criminally Investigated for Criticizing Public Official: Iván Cepeda

In 2007 the prosecutor's office in Sincelejo, Sucre department, in northwestern Colombia, initiated a criminal investigation against Iván Cepeda for allegedly committing criminal slander and libel.[149] Cepeda, a high-profile spokesperson for the National Movement for Victims of State Crimes, received Human Rights First's Roger Baldwin Medal of Liberty in 2007.[150] The investigation was the result of a formal complaint from José María Conde Romero, a congressman from Sucre in the House of Representatives.[151] Conde complained that Cepeda had criminally defamed him during a speech Cepeda made on November 27, 2006, at a public meeting in San Onofre, Sucre. After testimony from residents of links between public officials and paramilitary groups, Cepeda stated that Romero had connections with paramilitary groups.[152] Cepeda was describing what he considered, on the basis of testimonial evidence, to be public corruption and the involvement of a public official in potential human rights violations. The prosecutor did not investigate the allegations made by Cepeda or the veracity of his claims. Instead, he investigated Cepeda for criminal defamation. Human rights defenders, like all citizens, should not make false and spiteful statements against public officials. However, it is especially important that they should not feel constrained by the fear of criminal prosecution in speaking openly about the observance of human rights principles by state officials. While the Prosecutor General has taken the positive step of assigning the investigation of Cepeda to a new prosecutor in Bogotá, the case has not been closed.

VIII. Conclusions and Recommendations

"There is a problem of stigmatization of defenders... there are cases against defenders with clear political motivation... Defenders should not be charged for their work."

Carlos Franco, Presidential Human Rights Program[153]

PROSECUTORS IN COLOMBIA, as in any state, must investigate and prosecute crimes and ensure that perpetrators are brought to justice. However, those investigations must be conducted in accordance with both Colombian and international law. This report has revealed that investigations against defenders are frequently opened based either on fabricated, implausible evidence from witnesses lacking objectivity or on false, inadmissible intelligence reports. It has also revealed prosecutorial prejudice toward human rights defenders and the frequent use of arbitrary detention.

Because defenders are singled out for this type of persecution, solutions that focus specifically on defenders are needed. The recommendations below are designed to address each stage of the problem, from preliminary investigation to the arrest and detention of the defendant to the use of unreliable witnesses at trial. Concrete action on these recommendations will build on the recent changes in criminal procedures and on the professionalism and independence of some judges and prosecutors noted in this report, leading to a significant decrease in unfounded prosecutions.

A. Reviewing Investigations against Defenders

Colombian and international law contains fundamental tenets of due process that require prosecutors to vet accusations for plausibility at the preliminary investigation state, and then, before the accused is detained, gather independent evidence via an impartial investigation to corroborate such accusations. Where such verification reveals the accusation to be baseless, the investigation should be closed. Clearly, in cases that involve human rights defenders, these laws are being violated.

In many of the cases contained in this report, a more senior prosecutor or judge eventually dismissed the proceedings. However, the investigation should never have been initiated in the first place and the review of the proceedings should have occurred earlier. By the time the proceedings were closed, the defenders have already been stigmatized as rebels and terrorists and may face death threats and fear of attack for the rest of their lives. As the U.N. Working Group on Arbitrary Detention has pointed out in relation to Colombia, a subsequent prosecutorial review does not overcome the fact that the investigation was plagued by serious irregularities.[154] The fact that so many criminal investigations against defenders have been dismissed should not serve as validation that the justice system is working. Rather it demonstrates the widespread and endemic nature of the underlying problem.

Currently the process for reviewing prosecutions against defenders remains ad hoc and relies mainly on the ability of the defender to persistently lodge appeals and find an objective prosecutor. Therefore, there is a need for centralized coordination in order to guarantee that every investigation of a defender will be promptly and objectively reviewed. With centralized and trustworthy coordination, a prompt and objective review of the investigation is more likely. The existence of such a mechanism may in fact deter regional prosecutors from initiating spurious investigations in the first place. Specific action should include:

■ The Prosecutor General, or the prosecutors in charge of each case, should close the unfounded criminal investigations against the human rights defenders identified in this report.

■ The Prosecutor General should pass a resolution empowering his Human Rights Unit in Bogotá to coordinate the review of all criminal investigations against human rights defenders.[155] Its role should be similar to that which it currently assumes in relation to investigations of enforced disappearances. That Unit should be able to quickly vet the investigation for compliance with due process standards or rapidly delegate the review to the regional prosecutorial Human Rights Unit, if appropriate. All cases found to be specious should be closed immediately. Human rights defenders should be able to lodge complaints directly with the unit. In deciding which cases to review, the Human Rights Unit should adopt the broad definition of human rights defenders used by the U.N.[156]

■ The Inspector General's office should ensure that its judicial inspectors promptly and consistently intervene in cases of malicious prosecution of human rights defenders. Judicial inspectors should support the dismissal of specious charges against defenders.

U.S. appropriations legislation in 2008 earmarked $39.75 million in U.S. aid for judicial, human rights, rule of law, and related activities in Colombia, including $20 million for the Office of the Prosecutor General and $5 million for its Human Rights Unit.[157] Therefore:

■ USAID and the U.S. Department of Justice should support the Prosecutor General to enable the Human Rights Unit to monitor and review all criminal investigations against human rights defenders as envisioned in the second recommendation above. Such support could include funding, technical assistance, and training.

B. Addressing the Conduct of Prosecutors

Corruption among regional prosecutors contributes to the problem of malicious investigations, as does the failure of the Prosecutor General to investigate illegal conduct by prosecutors. Human Rights First is not aware of any disciplinary proceedings against or criminal investigations of any of the prosecutors who initiated the specious criminal investigations contained in this report. Moreover, judicial officials are either unaware of, or unwilling to abide by, the due process standards under international law and the Colombian Procedural Code. Prosecutors unduly influence witness statements or use patently false witness testimony. To address this aspect of specious prosecutions:

■ The Prosecutor General should conduct a comprehensive internal investigation into corruption and connections between justice officials and paramilitaries or successor groups, focusing on regional prosecutors. The state should dismiss from judicial and prosecutorial institutions all individuals shown to be corrupt or connected to illegal armed groups.

- The Prosecutor General should discipline and prosecute all prosecutors found to have breached the law in falsely investigating human rights defenders.

- Prosecutors should reject patently implausible witness testimony; refrain from influencing witness testimony and carefully evaluate witness testimony from ex-combatants who are receiving reintegration benefits. Prosecutors should also provide the accused with any evidence which may impeach the witness's credibility.

- The Prosecutor General should issue a resolution or directive addressed to all judicial and prosecutorial institutions reemphasizing relevant international law (cited in this report) and provisions of the new Colombian Procedural Code. The resolution should emphasize that these laws set standards for impartial investigations and fair trials and bar politically motivated criminal proceedings against human rights defenders and others.

C. Regulating Intelligence Reports

The armed forces and judicial police abuse the collection and use of information in intelligence reports, an integral part of the spurious prosecutions of defenders. The Inspector General and Ministry of Defense have already created a Working Group to establish criteria for the review of military intelligence files.[158] However, the Inspector General reports that the Defense Ministry and armed forces have not complied with the criteria established by that Working Group.[159] Most notably, the armed forces have reportedly not allowed the Inspector General to review intelligence files.[160] Instead, they have informed the Inspector General and Human Rights First that they have reviewed all files and that they contain no material relating to defenders.[161] The fact that the armed forces deny they have intelligence files relating to defenders when such

files are published in the media and used in judicial proceedings demonstrates the need for an independent authority to review those files.

The Colombian Congress should amend the *Intelligence and Counter-Intelligence Bill* before it to better regulate the collection and use of information in intelligence reports.[162] The legislation should:[163]

- Clarify that information may not be collected for arbitrary reasons, such as membership in a human rights organization;

- Unequivocally state that no intelligence report can be used as evidence in criminal or administrative proceedings;

- Include a requirement that judicial approval be obtained in order to collect intelligence;

- Empower the Inspector General to perform unannounced reviews of intelligence reports from any state institution to exclude all unfounded information that incriminates or is prejudicial to human rights defenders or others;[164]

- Prohibit the dissemination of information from intelligence reports;

- Uphold the right to *habeas data* (the ability of individuals to obtain and rectify information held about them) enshrined in the Colombian Constitution. The legislation should therefore establish a mechanism for individuals to access, verify, and correct information contained in intelligence reports;[165] and

- Establish a mechanism to verify that the above requirements are being respected and to prosecute officials who violate them.

D. Changing Prosecutorial Attitudes toward Human Rights Advocacy

Colombian society, and specifically prosecutors and judges, remains inappropriately suspicious of the nature of human rights advocacy. There are numerous instances of prosecutors equating the promotion of human rights with terrorism or subversive behavior. Some prosecutors, however, have pointed out that their colleagues should respect the legitimacy of human rights work. In dismissing an investigation against Julio Avella and other human rights defenders, a prosecutor found that the evidence showed that they were "good people who may profess a leftist ideology, which is permitted in a participatory and pluralist democracy such as ours."[166] Avella was coordinator of the Organization for the Defense and Promotion of Human Rights (REINICIAR) team in Santander (see Case 5, Annex). In closing the investigation against Alejandro Quiceno, a reviewing prosecutor stated, "To protest against the state is not a crime, because the opinions are respectable and protected by our Constitution. Every Colombian citizen has the right to dissent and to protest, which is a very different thing to carrying weapons of war and premeditating rebel acts."[167] See Case 28, Annex.

■ All Colombian public officials should refrain from making statements that discredit or stigmatize human rights defenders as guerrillas. The President should enact a new Presidential Directive to this effect, similar to those issued by previous administrations.[168]

■ As a major supporter of judicial reform in Colombia, the United States can play a constructive role. USAID should work with the Prosecutor General and the Ombudsman to implement an education program for prosecutors and judges concerning the value of human rights advocacy. The program should emphasize that human rights advocacy has

no connection with terrorism and is protected by Colombian and international law.

■ U.S. government officials should continue to raise individual cases of specious prosecutions of human rights defenders with their Colombian counterparts and emphasize that such persecution breaches the U.S. Guiding Principles on Non-Government Organizations. In addition, at the highest political levels, U.S. foreign policy should focus on structural reforms, contained in this report, to address the problem at a systemic level.

■ The U.S. Congress should include in appropriations legislation a condition requiring certification by the State Department that the Colombian armed forces are not involved in human rights violations against human rights defenders.

■ In certifying foreign assistance to Colombia under current appropriations legislation, the Department of State should consider the role the armed forces play in assisting malicious prosecutions of defenders.

■ The Department of State should end the practice of denying or revoking visas to Colombian human rights defenders based on the fact that they have been subject to a specious criminal prosecution or unfairly branded as a terrorist by public officials.

E. Decriminalizing Defamation and Slander

The criminal offenses of slander and libel are particularly susceptible to abuse and are frequently used to violate human rights defenders' freedom of expression. While legitimate as civil complaints, the Inter-American system for human rights has repeatedly stated that the criminalization of slander and libel breaches various rights protected by the American Convention on Human Rights.[169] In its most recent decision finding Argentina's criminal slander law in breach of the Convention, the

Inter-American Court of Human Rights held, "Opinion cannot be subject to legal penalties, especially when it involves a value judgment regarding an official act by a public official discharging his duties."[170]

A growing body of international law states that public officials should not enjoy protection from scrutiny. However, criminal libel laws are frequently used to prosecute human rights defenders for challenging public officials and therefore discourage scrutiny. The IACHR has stated, "Considering the consequences of criminal sanctions and the inevitable chilling effect they have on freedom of expression, criminalization of speech can only apply in those exceptional circumstances when there is an obvious and direct threat of lawless violence."[171] Other countries in the region have recently decriminalized libel and slander and converted them into civil complaints and Colombia should follow suit:[172]

- The Colombian Congress should amend the Colombian Criminal Code to decriminalize the offenses of slander and libel.

IX. Annex: Table of Individual Cases

	Defendant	Case Summary	Signs of Defects in the Investigation
1.	**Teofilo Acuña** President of Federation of Agro-Mining Unions in South Bolivar (*Federación Agrominera del Sur de Bolivar*, or FEDEAGROMISBOL). Acuña assists communities in opposing extraction of resources by multinational mining companies and has exposed alleged human rights violations of the New Granada Military Battalion.	Prosecutor 28 in Simiti arrested Acuña and charged him with rebellion on April 26, 2007, in Santa Rosa, Sur de Bolivar. He was detained in the Modelo Prison of Bucaramanga for ten days.	After ten days of detention, Acuña was released when the prosecutor's office admitted it did not have sufficient evidence to continue detaining him preventatively. The evidence against Acuña consisted of testimony from witnesses who lacked credibility and an intelligence file of unknown contents that was prepared by the New Granada Military Battalion. The Battalion was not an impartial source of information given that it was allegedly responsible for killing Acuña's predecessor at FEDEAGROMISBOL and had been the target of Acuña's human rights advocacy. Moreover, they were responsible for arresting Acuña and allegedly beating him. A reviewing prosecutor also found exculpatory evidence to undermine the reintegrated witnesses' testimonies and questioned their credibility based on the interests they had in benefits, security, and protection from the state and the army.
2.	**Oscar Duque, Mario Martinez, Evaristo Mena, Ramiro Ortega, Miguel Gonzalez, and Andres Gil** Board members of the Rural Association of Rio Valle del Rio Cimitarra (*Asociación Campesina del Valle del Rio Cimitarra,* or ACVC), a community organization that supports land access and development of the local economy.	Four of the ACVC leaders (Duque, Martinez, Mena, and Gil) were arrested in San Lorenzo del Municipio de Cantagallo by the army and in Barrancabermeja by the national police on September 29, 2007. The 3rd Prosecutorial Office in Bucaramanga charged them with rebellion. Gonzalez and Ortega were detained on January 19, 2008, by soldiers from the Calibío Battalion. All but Gonzalez and Gil were released in April and May 2008. Gonzalez and Gil remain detained and their trials have begun. Gil's trial is being prosecuted by the Prosecution Office of Medellín. Decisions in these two cases are expected in early 2009. Ortega was detained again in a raid on June 29, 2008, but held for only two hours.	The case has relied heavily on intelligence reports produced by the army and the DAS, which were not legally admissible as evidence. ACVC alleged that the authorities opened an investigation without notifying the defendants, depriving them of their right to defense and violating Colombian law. In April 2008, Prosecutor 37 of the Human Rights and International Law Unit in Medellin dismissed the charges against Duque, Martinez, and Mena. On May 19, Ortega was also freed. That prosecutor found that there was not sufficient evidence to hold them responsible for rebellion. He found that the intelligence reports lacked probative value because there was not proper corroboration. He also found that having communications with the FARC does not automatically mean that a person is involved in its activities given that civilians are frequently violently coerced and obliged to meet with guerrillas. Finally, the prosecutor found witness allegations were unreliable and lacked coherence and should have been verified in the preliminary investigation. However, the reviewing prosecutor did not close the investigation against Gonzalez and Gil, and failed to specify why they were more culpable.

	Defendant	Case Summary	Signs of Defects in the Investigation
3.	**Carmelo Agamez** Technical Secretary of the Movement of Victims of State Crimes (MOVICE) section in Sucre department. Granted protective measures from the Inter-American Commission on Human Rights (IACHR).	On November 13, 2008, five men in plainclothes who identified themselves as police raided Agamez's house. On November 15, 2008, he was arrested and jailed. Sincelejo prosecutors charged him with conspiracy to commit a crime with paramilitary forces, alleging that he participated in a paramilitary meeting in 2002. He was held in SIJIN custody for five days, and is currently detained at La Vega prison with the very paramilitary leaders he has denounced.	The initial raid against Agamez allegedly took place without a warrant, and Agamez was reportedly not notified of the charges against him for several days. Agamez's arrest happened shortly after he made a series of public denunciations of official corruption. The only evidence the prosecutor allegedly had is the uncorroborated testimony of two witnesses, one of whom was the wife of a mayor recently charged with corruption after MOVICE organized a public hearing. Agamez has received many threats from paramilitaries and appeared on a paramilitary "death list" in 2006. Given his strident opposition to paramilitary groups, it is implausible that he is also a paramilitary member.
4.	**Araucan defenders** The group of 18 human rights defenders, civil society leaders, and labor and social organizers detained in Arauca included **José Vicente Murillo Tobo**, President of the Joel Sierra Human Rights Committee in Arauca, and **Alonso Campiño Bedoya**, director of the Central Union for Workers Aracua Section (CUT). Both Murillo and Campiño had previously been granted protective measures by the IACHR.	Murillo and Campiño were detained along with 35 others, including many poor farmers, in Saravena, Arauca, on August 21, 2003. On February 24, 2004, the Special Prosecutor 12 from the National Terrorism Unit charged Murillo and Campiño with rebellion. On November 14, 2006, Murillo, Campiño and 17 others were found guilty by the Saravena Circuit Criminal Court in Bogotá. Their appeal has been pending before the Superior Tribunal of Arauca for over two years.	The defenders were detained in an allegedly violent raid by members of the CTI, DAS, and other government authorities. A judge decided to preventatively detain Murillo and Campiño but the prosecutor waited more than six months to officially charge them. The evidence compiled against Murillo and others consisted of uncorroborated testimony from witnesses who lacked credibility. The prosecutor and army apparently spent seven months coaching and preparing the testimony of two witnesses. The prosecutor has its base of operations within the 18th Brigade of the National Army, which may have compromised its independence, especially given Murillo's strident criticism of that unit.
5.	**Julio Avella** Coordinator of the Corporation for the Defense and Promotion of Human Rights (REINICIAR) team investigating human rights violations committed against the Patriotic Union political party in Santander. He is also director of National Association for Solidarity Assistance (ANDAS) and the Permanent Assembly of Civil Society.	Avella was detained on December 6, 2002, in Bucaramanga with six other defendants. On June 3, 2003, he was released after Prosecutor Rodrigo Rodriguez Barragan of Bucaramanga's Prosecutorial Unit 26 dismissed the charges.	The case relied on testimonies of reintegrated guerrillas and prejudicial intelligence reports by the CTI and RIME. In dismissing the case, Prosecutor Rodriquez held that the accusations were contradictory, incoherent, inconsistent, and illogical. The prosecutor found that Avella had been arrested for no more than his leftist ideology, with no evidence of rebellion or other wrongdoing.

	Defendant	Case Summary	Signs of Defects in the Investigation
6.	**Mauricio Avilez Alvarez** Coordinator of the Center for Studies and Development (CEDERNOS) and representative of the Human Rights Coordination Team in Barranquilla to Coordination Colombia-Europe- United States (CCEEUU).	On June 10, 2004, Avilez was detained by GAULA members affiliated with the Second Brigade of the First Division of the Army. He was accused of being a FARC guerilla by the 6th Specialist Prosecutor in Barranquilla. On October 20, 2004, the 4th Specialist Prosecutor before the Atlantico Criminal Court released him.	The prosecution relied on a sole witness, apparently an ex-FARC member, thought to have taken part in prosecutions against human rights defenders in other parts of Colombia. Use in unrelated proceedings calls into question the veracity of the witness's evidence. The credibility of the witness was further undercut by the army's reported admission that he was only testifying because he had been offered leniency in exchange for serving as an informant. The prosecutor allegedly did not receive the army intelligence report upon which Avilez's arrest was based or issue an arrest warrant until after he was detained.
7.	**Nicolas Castrillon** Vice-president of the Rural Association of Antioquia (ACA), member of Human Rights Collective Seeds of Liberty (CODEHSEL).	On November 14, 2005, Castrillon was detained in Bogotá by the National Police. SIJIN subsequently charged him with rebellion.	After interrogating him on November 18, 2005, the prosecutor concluded that Castrillón was innocent and ordered his immediate release, closing the investigation for lack of evidence. Castrillon was investigated along with Alejandro Quiceno (see below).
8.	**Teresa de Jesús Cedeño Galindez** Criminal defense attorney and former President of the Permanent Committee of Human Rights in Arauca (CPDH).	On July 30, 2003, the CTI detained Cedeño following a sting operation. She was originally charged by Prosecutor 287 in Bogotá with procedural fraud and bribery. The fraud charges were dropped quickly.	Cedeño appears to have been preventatively detained on the bribery charges alone, in breach of the Criminal Procedure Code. She was allegedly held for three days without access to her defense lawyers. The evidence against her was provided by reintegrated informants and the defense questioned the credibility of one witness who had been cited for false testimony before, and who took part in seven proceedings as a witness for the prosecution. The same witness misidentified information such as dates and names and his testimony was not corroborated. The prosecution or the CTI provided a video to the media that sought to publicly incriminate Cedeño. Military intelligence reports were used as evidence.
9.	**Iván Cepeda** Spokesperson for the National Movement for Victims of State Crimes (MOVICE) and awarded the 2007 Roger Baldwin Medal of Liberty by Human Rights First. Cepeda has precautionary measures from the IACHR and is in the Interior and Justice Ministry's protection program.	The 5th Delegate of the Prosecution Office in Sincelejo, Sucre, charged Cepeda with criminal slander and libel after a formal complaint by José Maria Conde Romero, a Congressman from Sucre in the Colombian House of Representatives.	The complaint against Cepeda was filed after he delivered a public speech in San Onofre, Sucre, on November 27, 2006, in which he expressed his opinion on the alleged connections between Congressman Conde and paramilitary groups. The Prosecutor General reassigned the investigation to a Bogotá-based prosecutor based on the lack of impartiality in the initial investigation in Sucre.

	Defendant	Case Summary	Signs of Defects in the Investigation
10.	**Juan Carlos Celis Gonzalez** Member of the Movement for Life in Bogotá.	Celis was detained on December 11, 2002, but was not charged until almost a year later, on November 27, 2003. The 13th Specialist Prosecutor from the Terrorism Unit in Bogotá charged him with rebellion and arms offenses. He was held in preventative detention for over two years in a maximum security prison far from his lawyer in Bogotá.	The prosecutor reportedly equated Gonzalez's human rights activities with support for the FARC. The main evidence for the charges was statements by witnesses who later claimed to have given incriminating evidence because they had been tortured by police. Celis also reported being beaten by police at the time of his arrest. It appears that no arrest warrant for Celis was ever issued.
11.	**Luz Perly Córdoba Mosquera** President of the Rural Association of Arauca (*Asociacion Campesina de Arauca* - ACA). She was in the Interior and Justice Ministry's protection program due to threats against her life and awarded protective measures by the IACHR in 2002. She was also manager of the human rights section of the Federation of National Farming Unions (FENSAUGRO).	Córdoba was arrested in Arauca by DAS members on February 18, 2004. Nearly six months later a prosecutor finally brought formal charges of rebellion and drug trafficking against Córdoba, which were annulled in March 15, 2005, by the 1st Criminal Court of the Arauca Specialized Circuit.	DAS reportedly alleged that the ACA was a political arm of the FARC and that Córdoba's human rights advocacy was a façade for terrorism and rebellion. The prosecutor also suggested that human rights advocacy is a part of the FARC's campaign to smear and discredit the Colombian nation. Photographs of Córdoba were apparently provided to each of the witnesses, violating established identification procedures. Córdoba's lawyer was allegedly detained at one point after visiting her in jail. Many of the witnesses apparently had significant criminal records and gave contradictory evidence yet the prosecutor reportedly made no attempts to determine their veracity.
12.	**Alfredo Correa de Andreis** Sociologist, Professor at University of Magdalena, University of Pavia Italy, University of Atlántico. At the time of his death he was conducting research on displacement and its effects on personal property and legal rights.	He was detained in Barranquilla on June 17, 2004, by the DAS of Bolivar, with support from the DAS Atlantico Barranquilla. He was accused of rebellion and of being a member of the FARC by the 33rd Prosecutor of Cartagena.	The case relied on a reintegrated guerrilla witness. He was released in July 2004 after a judge found no evidence against him. Shortly afterwards, on September 17, 2004, he was killed by paramilitaries. In April 2006, a former senior ranking official of the DAS reported that the DAS had provided to paramilitaries a "death list" in which Correa allegedly appeared.
13.	**Claudia Julieta Duque** Research journalist with focus on human rights violations. Worked with the José Alvear Restrepo Lawyers Collective to investigate crimes. Duque is now a consultant with UNICEF and has been granted asylum in Europe given the threats against her.	Duque was charged with criminal slander and libel by Prosecution Office 64 in Bogotá after a complaint by Emiro Rojas, a former Director of DAS in Antioquia.	Duque conducted groundbreaking research into the murder of fellow journalist Jaime Garzon and accused Rojas of irregularities in the murder investigation. It appears that the criminal slander charges were a direct response to her important human rights investigations and retaliation for her exposure of alleged human rights violations. They therefore interfere with her right to freedom of expression. The Constitutional Court held in 2008 that DAS breached her right to privacy because her DAS bodyguard compiled intelligence reports on her while supposedly providing her with protection.

	Defendant	Case Summary	Signs of Defects in the Investigation
14.	**Jesús Javier Dorado Rosero** Director of Permanent Committee of Human Rights (CPDH) in the Department of Nariño. Dorado was awarded protective measures from the Interior and Justice Ministry and the IACHR.	On May 26, 2005, Dorado was detained and imprisoned for four months and accused of rebellion by the Specialized Prosecutor 2 of El Pasto. After the Inspector General's office investigated the case, he was released. He was subsequently detained by DAS agents in the city of El Pasto on February 13, 2007.	A reviewing prosecutor and the Inspector General's office found the charges baseless. CPDH stated that the charges were politically motivated.
15.	**Diego Figueroa** Member of the Inter-Church Commission for Justice and Peace (CIJP). Agronomist, conducted clinics on nutrition, and assisted poor communities with food distribution in rural areas.	On November 28, 2005, Figueroa was arrested but released shortly thereafter. Prosecution Office 42 of Buenaventura again ordered his arrest on December 14, 2005, and charged him with rebellion. On June 20, 2006, the investigation was closed.	CIJP stated that in November 2005 Figueroa was detained without an arrest warrant, abused by the police, and denied access to his lawyer. The information later used as evidence of the crime of rebellion came from DAS reports filed during his November 2005 detention and from reintegrated witnesses who were unable to identify Figueroa. On June 20, 2006, Prosecutor 38 of Buenaventura dismissed the investigation, finding that the reintegrated witness testimonies had flaws and did not demonstrate any criminal activity committed by Figueroa.
16.	**Elizabeth Gomez and Luz Marina Arroyabe** Members of the Inter Church Commission for Justice and Peace (CIJP). Gomez and Arroyabe assist communities in Curvaradó and Jiguamiandó to peacefully reclaim land illegally appropriated.	Gomez and Arroyabe were preventatively detained on May 17, 2008, by the Police Inspector of Riosucio and charged with violent association and attempting a coup (*asonada*). On May 18 2008, Prosecutor 15 of Riosucio, Choco dismissed the charges and released them.	Upon investigating the charges against Gomez and Arroyabe, Prosecutor 15 of Riosucio found that there were insufficient grounds for preventative detention and released them. At the time of their detention, they were not informed of the charges against them and were allegedly asked to sign documents without the presence of an attorney. The defense attorney was reportedly not given access to their files, potentially violating the right to defense (articles 8 and 13 of the Criminal Procedural Code).
17.	**Principe Gabriel Gonzalez** Regional Coordinator of the Political Prisoners Solidarity Committee (CSPP) in Santander. Student leader at Industrial University of Santander (UIS). Former Human Rights Secretary for the National Student Federation.	Gonzalez was detained in Pamplona and held in Modelo prison, Bucaramanga, Santander, from January 4, 2006, to April 4, 2007. He was charged with rebellion by the 21st Division of the Bucaramanga Prosecution Office. Judge José Alberto Pabon Ordoñez of the 8th Criminal Circuit in Bucaramanga acquitted him on March 30, 2007. That decision was appealed by the prosecutor and judicial inspector. Nearly two years later the case is still pending.	Judge Pabon found that the charges against Gonzalez were unfounded and relied on evidence that lacked impartiality and credibility. The judge recognized that the legal system was being manipulated and dismissed witness evidence in part "due to the fear that [the witness's] evidence was being used to direct the judicial system against those who are fighting for social or democratic causes or claiming their rights." The only other witness in the case told the CSPP that her statements were made under duress from members of the police and the CTI in Bucaramanga. Furthermore, the prosecution reportedly publicized photos of González via prominent media outlets as an alleged guerrilla member before the witness had even identified him in a line-up, thereby calling into question the subsequent positive identification. The judge also found that the prosecutor had a discriminatory attitude to human rights defenders in general and may have fabricated elements of the offense.

	Defendant	Case Summary	Signs of Defects in the Investigation
18.	**Hernando Hernandez** Indigenous leader and member of the Permanent Committee for the Defense of Human Rights, in Caldas. Member of FENSUAGRO. Granted preventative measures by the Inter-American Court of Human Rights and asylum in Spain.	Hernandez was detained by DAS on June 1, 2005, in Bogotá and later transferred to the city of Manizales. He was accused of rebellion but released on November 28, 2005, by the Prosecutor General's Terrorism Unit.	DAS agents allegedly denied they had Hernandez in their custody until a *habeas corpus* petition was filed. The 7th Prosecution Office of Manizales subsequently ordered preventative detention measures. Information of his arrest was given to the local press and an article accusing him of being a member of the FARC was published, stigmatizing him publicly. After six months, the Prosecutor General's Terrorism Unit closed the investigation, citing lack of sufficient evidence.
19.	**Victor Julio Laguado Boada** Agrarian social leader in Arauca. Has held various leadership positions in the agricultural cooperative COAGROSARARE.	Laguado was charged with rebellion by the National Anti-Terrorism Unit in October 2006. He was pronounced absent from the proceedings on February 12, 2007, after they were transferred to Bogotá. In May 2007 he was preventatively detained.	The case relied on reintegrated witness testimonies and two intelligence reports from the National Police of Arauca. Moreover, the prosecutor's independence was compromised given its location within the headquarters of the Army's 18th Brigade. The testimony provided by two reintegrated witnesses was inconsistent and contradictory and appeared copied from the intelligence reports, which were made well before the witnesses testified. Laguados's detention was set against a backdrop of widespread detentions in Arauca.
20.	**Aldemar Lozano** Community leader for the Inter-Church Commission for Justice and Peace (CIJP) and former president of the council of community action of Puerto Esperanza.	On November 24, 2007, Lozano was detained in Mosquera, Bogotá, by members of DIJIN and released on November 25, 2007, by a judge in Madrid, Cundina-marca, in an oral hearing.	Lozano was allegedly detained without being informed of his rights or the nature of the charges against him. He was later accused of trafficking in illegal materials. A judge declared his arrest illegal after finding the evidence irrelevant and that the defense had proved his innocence.
21.	**Nieves Mayuza** Member of the National Federation of Agricultural Farming Unions (FENSUAGRO). **Carmen Mayuza** Regional leader of the Association of Health and Social Security Workers of Colombia (ANTHOC).	Both sisters were arrested on May 11, 2006, charged with rebellion, and accused of being members of the 53rd Front of the FARC. They were released in June 2008.	On June 18, 2008, Judge Arrieta, from Court 53 of the Bogotá Criminal Circuit, acquitted them of all charges (along with Fanny Perdomo Hite, see Case 26). Judge Arrieta held that: the investigation was too subjective and ignored clear exculpatory evidence; the evidence was unfounded; and that GAULA had no expertise to investigate this case. Furthermore, a judicial inspector found that the minimum substantial requirements to accuse them were not met and that substantial evidence of responsibility, not mere suspicions, was necessary.
22.	**Alfredo Molano** Investigative writer, sociologist, journalist for the *Espectador* newspaper.	Criminal charges for libel and slander were initiated by the General Prosecution Office before the 4th Municipal Criminal Court of Bogotá.	The Araujo de Valledupar family filed criminal charges against Molano for libel and slander based on the publication of the article "Araujos et al" in *El Espectador* on February 24, 2007. Molano expressed his critical opinion about certain acts of alleged corruption against the community of Valledupar. Molano may face imprisonment if found guilty.

	Defendant	Case Summary	Signs of Defects in the Investigation
23.	**Claudia Montoya** Lawyer for the Young Person's Network of Medellín. Represents juveniles illegally detained and physically abused by public authorities.	The former Provincial Inspector General for the Valley of Aburra, Adriana Cecilia Martinez, brought a disciplinary process against Montoya, but on July 8, 2005, it was dismissed. On October 18, 2006, CTI members and police arrested Montoya and charged her with rebellion. She was preventively detained until December 2006, when a reviewing prosecutor found that the detention was illegal. However, Montoya remained under house arrest. The charges against her were dismissed on February 9, 2007, and she was released after almost four months of detention.	In overturning the preventive detention order against Montoya, a prosecutor found the testimonies of witnesses vague and reliant on hearsay information. The witnesses were not able to accurately describe or identify Montoya as the supposed guerrilla referred to in a CTI intelligence report, which lacked sufficient information or strong supporting evidence to accuse Montoya. That prosecutor found that criminal charges against human rights defenders are often false and must be reviewed with caution. Moreover, that prosecutor also stated that the witnesses had been led by the initial prosecutor, who named Montoya as the accused before witnesses had identified her. Some witness statements were worded almost identically, suggesting interference and coaching by the initial prosecutor. The initial prosecutor also failed in its duty to investigate exculpatory evidence, such as the fact that a university corroborated Montoya's attendance.
24.	**Amaury Padilla** Works for the Association for Alternative Social Promotion (MINGA), Bogotá At the time of his detention he was a director in the office of the Governor of Bolivar department liaising with the U.N. and NGOs and had a high profile in the human rights movement.	Padilla was arrested on December 26, 2003, and charged with rebellion by Prosecutor 33 of the Reaction Unit. He was investigated by Prosecutor 39 of the Unit specializing in crimes against public health and safety in Cartagena. He was detained until July 4, 2004, when the Prosecutor General's office closed the investigation.	Four of the five witnesses that testified against Padilla were reintegrated guerrillas. The Prosecutor General found that the Prosecution failed to corroborate the testimonies and investigate exculpatory evidence. Also, he found that the testimonies were inconsistent, contradictory and lacked credibility. The Prosecutor General concluded that some of the witnesses were coached since their testimonies were identical. There were also irregularities in the process of taking the depositions such as reliance on transcripts instead of interrogations in person. Moreover, the procedure of photo identification was suggestive and flawed.
25.	**Rafael Palencia** Human Rights Professor and founder of the Permanent Committee of Human Rights (CPDH) in Bolivar. Advocate for political prisoners. Coordinator of trainings and workshops about the International Criminal Court with the International Federation of Human Rights.	Palencia was charged with rebellion after being detained on February 19, 2003, in Cartagena. He was held for 14 months, after which he was released for lack of evidence. On November 20, 2006, his house was raided by DAS at the order of the 5th Prosecutor of the Immediate Reaction Unit in Barranquilla.	The prosecution's case against Palencia relied heavily on accusations of a witness who lived in an area controlled by paramilitary forces and whose objectivity was questioned. The investigation coincided with the publication of a SIJIN intelligence report that reportedly labeled Palencia and others as FARC lawyers. After his initial detention, Palencia moved to Bogotá, fearful for his security. Beginning in July 2006, Palencia stated that his house was monitored by State agents and he was briefly detained on July 9, 2006, which prompted him to move again. In the November 2006 raid, DAS confiscated documents and computers from Palencia. The U.N. Special Rapporteur on Human Rights Defenders expressed concern that his detention was related to his human rights advocacy.

	Defendant	Case Summary	Signs of Defects in the Investigation
26.	**Fanny Perdomo Hite** Member of the Citizens' Community for Life and Peace, a group of displaced citizens working to reclaim their land without intervention of members of the armed conflict.	Perdomo was arrested on May 11, 2006, on suspicion of kidnapping and rebellion. The kidnapping charges were quickly dropped by the prosecution. She was tried for rebellion by the 9th Prosecutor of the Anti-Kidnapping and Extortion Unit in Bogotá and acquitted of the charges on June 18, 2008, by a Judge on the 53rd Criminal Court in Bogotá.	Perdomo was detained after GAULA wiretapped her phone lines to start an investigation for kidnapping. Judge Arrieta found Perdomo innocent in June 2008. She found that the evidence was insufficient and that Perdomo had merely provided personal gifts to her sister, which did not constitute criminal activity. Furthermore, the judge questioned the credibility and expertise of the author of the GAULA intelligence report. She also questioned the credibility of the military intelligence report that formed the basis of the conviction of Perdomo's sister. Finally, the judge found exculpatory evidence and held that the presumption of innocence had not been overcome.
27.	**Elkin de Jesús Ramirez** Lawyer and Professor at the University of Antioquia, Medellin. Legal Advisor and Human Rights Educator with the Legal Liberty Organization (CJL).	Prosecutor 74 in the Antioquia Prosecutor's Office issued an arrest warrant against Ramirez on November 29, 2006, for the crime of rebellion, but it was allegedly rescinded before being executed. The rebellion investigation against him was dismissed in 2008 by a reviewing prosecutor. A case of criminal defamation was earlier filed by a colonel of the Army's 17th Brigade in 2005, but it was dismissed because no evidence of criminal wrongdoing was produced.	The prosecution did not notify Ramirez of the ongoing investigation against him until his arrest, and the existence of the investigation was allegedly denied by judicial authorities in meetings with the U.N. High Commissioner for Human Rights. A reviewing prosecutor dismissed the rebellion case after finding that the testimonies against Ramirez were incoherent, illogical, unreasonable, contradictory, and vague. According to the reviewing prosecutor, the witnesses used similar phrases in their declarations, which may have been an indicator of previous preparation. He also found that the documents and wiretapped conversations provided as evidence against Ramirez were irrelevant and did not demonstrate his involvement with the FARC. The initial prosecutor failed to act on exculpatory evidence such as testimonies of University of Antioquia faculty. The prosecutor also stated that the reintegrated witnesses may have given biased testimonies against Ramirez in order to obtain economic benefits from the government.
28.	**Alejandro Quiceno** Human rights activist in Medellin with Sumapaz Human Rights Foundation, Seeds of Liberty Human Rights Collective, and the Legal Liberty Organization (CJL).	Quiceno was detained on March 30, 2005, and charged with rebellion by the 5th Specialized Prosecutor in Medellin. He was detained for over three months despite a bail application that apparently met statutory requirements. He was subsequently sent to house arrest. On September 19, 2005, Prosecutor 153 of Medellin found the detention unjustified and ordered his release.	Reviewing the case, Prosecutor 153 of Medellin found the testimonies of reintegrated witnesses unreliable as they were seeking benefits from the government. She found that Quiceno was involved in legitimate human rights advocacy that was legal and quite distinct from rebellion. The prosecutor held that the period of six months for a preliminary investigation had been violated.

	Defendant	Case Summary	Signs of Defects in the Investigation
29.	**Martin Sandoval** President of the Permanent Committee of Human Rights in Arauca (CPDH). Sandoval was detained with 15 other social and union leaders from Arauca including Guillermo Diaz, Adan José Castellanos, Alberto Vanegas, Olegario Araque, Santiago Gómez, Gonzalo Losada, Carlos Botero, José Santos Ortiz, José Vicente Leon, Samuel Guillen, Joaquin Vanegas.	The group was detained in an operation by the CTI, DAS, and National Police on November 4, 2008. Prosecutor Ruth Tovar Merchan of the 1st Specialist Prosecutor's Unit in Cucuta and Arauca apparently authorized the detention, accusing the defenders of rebellion. On November 5, they were transferred to Aracuta by the 18th Brigade of the Army.	Sandoval's detention appears related to his human rights advocacy. He has criticized the government's human rights record in Arauca, especially on such issues as arbitrary detention, forced displacement, and extrajudicial executions. Sandoval has previously been detained by the National Police and army, allegedly due to his human rights advocacy. On July 31, 2008, Sandoval and members of the Workers Union of SINTRAOVA publicly denounced the persecution against them in a hearing held by the House of Representative's Human Rights Commission. On October 23, the 5th Brigade of the National Army detained ten farm workers in Arauca affiliated with the Rural Association of Arauca. That same day, CPDH and other NGOs in Arauca received death threats in an email purportedly sent by paramilitaries.
30.	**Diana Teresa Sierra** A human rights lawyer at *Humanidad Vigente*, an organization that represents and supports victims of human rights violations in rural areas such as Arauca and Magdalena Medio. Sierra was formerly a lawyer with the Inter-Church Commission for Justice and Peace (CIJP), representing defenders accused of rebellion such as Fanny Perdome (see Case 26).	On November 20, 2007, Prosecutor 32 of Medellin filed a disciplinary complaint against Sierra with the Regional Judicial Council of Antioquia.	Prosecutor Gloria Ines Salazar alleged that Sierra acted "recklessly and with bad faith in trying to lead the proceedings" disrespecting her authority. On July 31st, 2008, the Disciplinary Tribunal of Antioquia terminated the investigation, dismissing the complaint. Judge Hernandez Quiñónez stated that Sierra had not obstructed the administration of justice and that the complaint was a waste of the court's time: "In the actions of the lawyer [Sierra] by no means can an obstruction to the administration of justice be inferred, being doubtful all the matters raised by the judicial official. It is lamentable that the administration of justice is worn down with complaints such as this."
31.	**Luis Torres** Former President of the Association of Displaced People from Salado Bolivar (ASODESBOL).	Torres was arrested May 26, 2005, by the CTI in Cartagena. He was accused of rebellion and belonging to the FARC. He was released on June 8, 2005 by Prosecutor 36 Ricardo Carriazo Zapata.	The only evidence against him was reintegrated witness testimony, which alleged that Torres gave information to the guerrilla resulting in the death of two people. However, one of the people who supposedly died subsequently came forward to testify. The Prosecution Office in Cartagena thought it was necessary to change the prosecutor assigned to the case. Prosecutor Carriazo of the special unit of rebellion in Cartagena found that the evidence was not enough to order preventive detention.

	Defendant	Case Summary	Signs of Defects in the Investigation
32.	**Hector Hugo Torres** President of the Human Rights and International Humanitarian Law Commission of Bajo Ariari.	Torres was charged with rebellion and association to commit a crime by the 1st Specialized Prosecutor Miguel Farid Polania Martinez of Villavicencio and detained by SIJIN agents on December 26, 2007 in Bosa, Bogotá. On December 27, the 6th Municipal Criminal Court in Villavicencio declared his detention illegal and released him.	The case was based on testimonies of reintegrated witnesses. Judge Luz Yolanda Sierra de Vargas found that the witnesses against Torres were coached and that the preparation of testimonies is a common practice used in different judicial proceedings to incriminate innocent civilians. He said that these "professional witnesses" live in military properties and receive economic and judicial benefits as rewards for their declarations. The judge also found that Torres' rights to defense and due process were violated. Torres reported being followed two days after being released, which he took to be a form of intimidation.

X. Endnotes

[1] On October 29, 2004, the Inter-American Commission on Human Rights (IACHR) granted precautionary measures in favor of Francisco Ramírez. Precautionary measures are only awarded to protect life and personal integrity in "serious and urgent cases... to prevent irreparable harm to persons." IACHR, *Rules of Procedure of the Inter-American Commission on Human Rights*, Approved at 109 Special Session, December 4-8, 2000 and subsequently amended, art. 25. The IACHR described him as "a prominent attorney known for his investigative work and defense of the rights of workers and indigenous communities, campesinos, and Afro-Colombians." IACHR, "Precautionary Measures 2004: Precautionary Measures Granted or Extended by the Commission," October 29, 2004, available at http://www.iachr.org/medidas/2004.eng.htm

[2] Claudia Montoya Case, Third Prosecutor Medellín Hernando Betancur, *Resolution Resolving Appeal*, Medellin, Third Prosecution Office, Superior Tribunal of Antioquia, December 6, 2005, p. 5.

[3] Hina Jilani, *Report of the Special Representative of the Secretary-General on Human Rights Defenders, Commission on Human Rights*, 58th session (New York: United Nations, April 2002), U.N. Doc: E/CN.4/2002/106/Add.2. 24. p. 24-25.

[4] Luis Camilo Osorio Isaza, Prosecutor General, *Resolution No 0-1678*, May 3, 2005.

[5] Human Rights First interview with Guillermo Mendoza, Colombian Deputy Attorney General, Bogotá, November 7, 2007.

[6] Human Rights First interview with Danilo Rueda, Director, Inter-Church Commission for Justice and Peace, November 21, 2008.

[7] Organization of American States, Tenth Report of the Secretary General to the Permanent Council on the MAPP/OAS Mission, October 31, 2007, OAS Doc No. CP/doc.4249/07; International Crisis Group, *Colombia's New Armed Groups*, May 10, 2007, Latin America Report N°20.

[8] For a more detailed description of human rights defenders, see United Nations Office of the High Commissioner for Human Rights, *Human Rights Defenders: Protecting the Right to Defend Human Rights, Fact Sheet No. 29* (Geneva: United Nations, 2004), pp. 2- 8.

[9] FIDH and OMCT: The Observatory for the Protection of Human Rights Defenders, *Colombia Las Tinieblas de la Impunidad: Muerte y Persecución a los Defensores de Derechos Humanos*, November 2006; See also Asamblea Permanente de la Sociedad Civil por la Paz et al, *Informe para el Examen Periódico Universal de Colombia*, July 2008, p. 8.

[10] See Human Rights First, Front Line, FIDH and OMCT, *Joint Submission for Universal Periodic Review: Colombia*, July 18, 2008, available at http://www.humanrightsfirst.info/pdf/080718-HRD-hrf-fl-omct-fidh-colombia-upr.pdf. *See also* Peace Brigades International, *Colompbia: Quarterly Newsletter*, No. 6, March 2008.

[11] Colombian Criminal Code, Law 599 of 2000, Official Diary No 44.097, July 24, 2000.

[12] See Human Rights First, *Losing Ground: Human Rights Defenders and Counterterrorism in Thailand*, 2006; Human Rights First, *Reformasi & Resistance: Human Rights Defenders & Counterterrorism in Indonesia*, 2005; Human Rights First, *Karimov's War: Human Rights Defenders and Counterterrorism in Uzbekistan*, 2005; and Human Rights First, *The New Dissidents: Human Rights Defenders and Counterterrorism in Russia*, 2005.

[13] Colombian Commission of Jurists, "University Community Submitted to Absurd Inquisition," press release, November 12, 2008. The order was made on November 10, 2008, by Prosecutor Jorge Iván Piedrahita Montoya of the Prosecutor General's Terrorism Unit and related to the following universities: Distrital, Pedagogica, Libre, Universidad Nacional and Servicio Nacional de Aprendizaje .

[14] David Campuzano, "Clara Lopez Obregon fue 'Chuzada' por la Fiscalia," *El Espectador*, November 27, 2008.

[15] Center for International Policy, "When Arbitrary Arrests Become Death Sentences," October 17, 2004, available at http://www.ciponline.org/colombia/blog/archives/000013.htm. Correa's sister told the newspaper *El Espectador*,"They didn't kill Alfredo on Friday. They really killed him when they arrested him. That was the day they placed the tombstone over him." *See also* Center for International Policy, "The DAS Scandals," April 13, 2006 available at http://www.ciponline.org/colombia/blog/archives/000242.htm

[16] For more information see the Protection Program's website: http://www.mininteriorjusticia.gov.co/pagina1.asp?doc=152

[17] Human Rights First, "Demand End to Baseless Prosecutions against Colombian Activists," October 15, 2008, available at http://www.humanrightsfirst.org/defenders/hrd_colombia/alert101508_giraldo_colom.html

[18] In 2003, the Inter-American Commission on Human Rights issued precautionary measures on behalf of the organization, finding that "they have been subject to threats, have been followed, have [been] subject to accusations, have been subject to repeated detentions and searches since 1997, and more intensely since the first half of 2003, as part of a pattern of conduct aimed at thwarting or hindering its work on behalf of human rights in the

regions of Colombia in which it accompanies especially vulnerable communities." IACHR, *Precautionary Measures 2003: Measures Granted or Extended by the Commission*, September 8, 2003.

[19] For a full list and citations see Human Rights First, *Colombia's Human Rights Defenders in Danger: Case Studies of Unfounded Criminal Investigations against Human Rights Defenders*, September 2007, available at http://www.humanrightsfirst.info/pdf/07906-hrd-colombia-whiite-paper.pdf , p 3.

[20] *Ibid.*

[21] *See for example*, Human Rights First, Front Line, FIDH And OMCT, *Joint Submission for Universal Periodic Review: Colombia*, July 18, 2008, available at http://www.humanrightsfirst.info/pdf/080718-HRD-hrf-fl-omct-fidh-colombia-upr.pdf; Human Rights First, "Stop Arbitrary Detention of Colombian Activists," January 31, 2008, available at http://www.humanrightsfirst.org/defenders/hrd_colombia/alert013108_TorresH.htm; Human Rights First, "Drop Baseless Charges against Colombian Human Rights Leader," June 1, 2007, available at http://www.humanrightsfirst.org/defenders/hrd_colombia/alert060107_cepeda.htm ; Human Rights First, Call for Release of Imprisoned Colombian Human Rights Leaders, January 17, 2007, available at http://www.humanrightsfirst.org/defenders/hrd_colombia/alert011707_gonzales.htm; Human Rights First, "Demand Release of Detained Colombian Activist," December 2, 2008, available at http://action.humanrightsfirst.org/campaign/Agamez

[22] Human Rights First interviews with the Vice-President, President of the Supreme Court, Presidential Adviser on Human Rights, Deputy Attorney-General, Vice-President of the Senate Human Rights Commission, and high ranking officials from the Interior and Justice Ministry, Ombudsman's office, Inspector-General's office, Office of the U.N. High Commissioner for Human Rights (OHCHR), and U.S. Embassy, Bogota, November 5 to November 13, 2007.

[23] Human Rights First interview with Guillermo Mendoza, Deputy Attorney-General, Sandra Castro Ospina, Head of the Human Rights Unit; and Francisco Echeverri, International Affairs, November 7, 2007. Mendoza invited Human Rights First to present him with a report that demonstrated that the problem was pervasive rather than consisting of only isolated cases.

[24] *See* Human Rights First, *What Is a Fair Trial? A Basic Guide to Legal Standards and Practice*, March 2000, available at http://www.humanrightsfirst.org/pubs/descriptions/fair_trial.pdf; Human Committee, *General Comment 13, Article 14* (Twenty-first session, 1984), Compilation of General Comments and General Recommendations Adopted by Human Rights Treaty Bodies, U.N. Doc. HRI/GEN/1/Rev.6 at 135 (2003).

[25] Colombia ratified the ICCPR on October 29, 1969, and it came into force on March 23, 1976. The ACHR entered into force on November 22,1969.

[26] Adopted by the Eighth United Nations Congress on the Prevention of Crime and the Treatment of Offenders, Havana, Cuba, August 27 to September 7, 1990.

[27] United Nations, *General Assembly Resolution*, U.N. Doc. A/45/49 (1990) 45/111, Annex, 45 U.N. GAOR Supp. (No. 49A) p. 200, New York.

[28] United Nations, *Guidelines on the Role of Prosecutors*, 1990, Adopted by the Eighth United Nations Congress on the Prevention of Crime and the Treatment of Offenders.

[29] ICCPR, article 19; ACHR, article 13.

[30] United Nations, Declaration on the Right and Responsibility of Individuals, Groups and Organs of Society to Promote and Protect Universally Recognized Human Rights and Fundamental Freedoms, December 9, 1998, A/RES/53/144, art 6(c).

[31] Colombian Criminal Procedural Code, Law 600 of 2000, Official Diary No. 44.097, July 24, 2000, art. 397.

[32] For more information see: Prosecutor General, *Manual of Procedural Law of the Prosecutor General in the Accusatory Criminal System in Colombia* (Bogota: 2005).

[33] Colombian Criminal Procedural Code, Law 906 of 2004, September 1, 2004, Official Diary No 45.658.

[34] Colombian Criminal Procedural Code, Law 600 of 2000, July 24, 2000, Official Diary No 44.097.

[35] Ibid, art. 237. See also article 232, which states that, "every decision must be based on legal evidence and regular and timely allegations. A guilty sentence cannot be passed without evidence that shows the certainty of the punishable conduct and the responsibility of the accused."

[36] Presidential Press Secretary, "NGO Guiding Principles in the United States Coincide with Criteria of President Uribe," press release, April 30, 2007 available at http://www.presidencia.gov.co/prensa_new/sne/2007/abril/30/11302007.htm

[37] U.S. State Department Bureau of Democracy, Human Rights, and Labor, *Guiding Principles on Non-Governmental Organizations*, December 14, 2006. Principle 3 states,"NGOs should be permitted to carry out their peaceful work in a hospitable environment free from fear of harassment, reprisal, intimidation and discrimination."

[38] Colombian Minister of National Defense, *Defense Ministry Directive 9 of 2003: Policies of Defense Ministry with respect to the protection of human rights, union leaders and human rights defenders*; President of the Republic, *Presidential Directive 7 of 1999: Support, Exchange and Collaboration of the State with Human Rights Organizations*, September 9, 1999; President of the Republic, *Presidential Directive 7 of 2001: Support, Exchange and Collaboration of the State with Human Rights Organizations that Develop Humanitarian Activities in the Country*, November 21, 2001.

[39] Decree 128 of 2003, January 22, 2003, implements a legal framework consisting of Law 418 of 1997, Official Gazette No. 43201, December 26, 1997, and Law 782 of 2002, Official Gazette No. 4043, December 23, 2002.

[40] See e.g., Constitutional Court, Decision C-392–00, Judge Antonio Barrera Carbonell, April 6, 2000; *Decision of First Instance*, 8th Criminal Circuit, Bucaramanga, Process 2006-0179-00, Judge José Alberto Pabon Ordóñez , March 30, 2007, p. 5.

[41] Art 13. of Decree 128 allows those who demobilize to receive pardons and other legal benefits for "political and related offenses" so long as they have not been investigated or convicted of crimes such as terrorism, genocide or murder committed outside combat (Law 782, art. 19). Given high impunity levels in Colombia, the vast majority of members of armed groups who have committed such acts have not been investigated or convicted of those crimes so they can avail themselves of the benefit scheme. Those who obtain these benefits may not in the future be prosecuted in relation to the same facts giving rise to the granting of benefits (Law 418, art. 62).

[42] *Judgment at Second Instance*, Superior Tribunal, Judge Luis Edgar Albarracin Posada, September 12, 2005.

[43] Ibid.

[44] Human Rights First interview with Guillermo Mendoza, Deputy Attorney General, Bogotá, November 7, 2007.

[45] Prosecutor 37, Human Rights and International Humanitarian Unit of Medellín, *Resolution of Dismissal*, April 23, 2008.

[46] Lucia Giraldo Prosecutor 153, Unit for Offenses against the Constitutional Regime, *Resolution of Dismissal* September 19, 2005, p. 16.

[47] Arger Londoño Sonson, Prosecutor 120 before the Criminal Circuit, *Resolution of Dismissal*, January 15, 2008, p. 5.

[48] Ibid.

[49] Prosecutor Beatriz Osorio, Santa Barbara, *Resolution of Dismissal*, February 9, 2007, p. 3-4.

[50] Third Prosecutor Medellín Hernando Betancur, *Resolution Resolving Appeal*, December 6, 2005, p. 2.

[51] Prosecutor-General's Supreme Court Unit, *Resolution Closing Investigation of Amaury Enrique Padilla Cabarcas*, File No 8278, June 3, 2004, p. 37.

[52] Ibid.

[53] For more information about Príncipe Gabriel González, see http://www.humanrightsfirst.org/defenders/hrd_colombia/hrd_González.asp; see also Human Rights First, *Colombia's Human Rights Defenders in Danger*.

[54] *Decision of First Instance*, 8th Criminal Circuit Bucaramanga, Process 2006-0179-00, Judge José Alberto Pabon Ordóñez, March 30, 2007, p. 10.

[55] Political Prisoners Solidarity Committee (CSPP), *Memorandum to Human Rights First about González case*; See also Amnesty International. *Colombia: Fear and Intimidation: The Dangers of Human Rights Work*, 2006, AI Index: AMR 23/033/2006, p. 14.

[56] Ibid., p. 45. The Prosecutor General also criticized the fact that DAS officers showed witnesses a photo of Padilla with his name printed on it, before they had identified a perpetrator. Ibid., p 9.

[57] For more information see Human Rights First, "Stop Arbitrary Detention of Colombian Activists," January 31, 2008.

[58] *Decision of Second Municipal Criminal Court of Villavicencio*, Judge Luz Yolanda Sierra de Vargas, December 27, 2007.

[59] Tito Augusto Gaitan, *Defense Brief to Maria Cristina Ramirez, Judges of Saravena Criminal Circuit: Support of the Appeal of the Unjust Decision of against Araucan Human Rights Defenders and Social Leaders*, File No. 2004-298, 2007.

[60] Ibid.

[61] Ibid.

[62] Pabon, *Decision of First Instance*, p. 7.

[63] Ibid., p. 10.

[64] See case summary for Elkin Ramirez.

[65] Arger Londoño Sonson Prosecutor 120 before the Criminal Circuit, *Resolution of Dismissal*, January 15, 2008, p. 5.

[66] Inter-American Commission on Human Rights, *Precautionary Measures 2000: Precautionary Measures Granted or Extended by the Commission*, November 1, 2000, available at http://www.iachr.org/medidas/2000.eng.htm

[67] Rural Association of Rio Cimitarra Valley (ACVC), "Three directors of the Campesino Association of the Valley of the River Cimitarra arrested," press release, September 30, 2007, p. 1, available at http://prensarural.org/spip/spip.php?article696

[68] Rural Association of Rio Cimitarra Valley (ACVC), "Two Other ACVC Leaders Captured," press release, January 20, 2008, p. 2 available at http://prensarural.org/spip/spip.php?article973

[69] Prosecutor 37, Human Rights and International Humanitarian Unit of Medellín, *Resolution of Dismissal*, April 23, 2008.

[70] Ibid.

[71] Prosecutor-General's Supreme Court Unit, *Resolution Closing Investigation of Amaury Enrique Padilla Cabarcas*, File No 8278, June 3, 2004 p 44.

[72] Ibid, p 42.

[73] Human Rights First interview with Gustavo Gallon, Colombian Commission of Jurists, Bogota, November 8, 2007.

[74] Article 50, Law 504 of 1999, June 29 1999, Official Diary No 43.618.

[75] Constitutional Court, Decision C-392-00, Judge Antonio Barrera Carbonell, April 6, 2000; *See also* the following Constitutional Court decisions supporting this principle: Decision C-1315-00, Judge Álvaro Tafur Galvis, September 26, 2000; Decision C-793-00, Judge Vladimiro Naranjo Mesa, June

29, 2000. *See also* Supreme Court of Justice, *Sentence of 25 May 1999*, Magistrate Carlos Eduardo Mejia Escobar, No: 12.885; *Sentence of 20 June 2001*, Magistrate Álvaro Orlando Perez Pinzon.

[76] Constitutional Court, Decision, T-066–98, Judge Eduardo Cifuentes Munoz.

[77] Human Rights First, "Community member killed while fishing," November 9, 2006 , available at http://www.humanrightsfirst.org/defenders/hrd_colombia/alert110906_sarmiento.htm

[78] Network of Solidarity, "Urgent Action: Detained President of Federation Agrominera of South Bolivar," April 26, 2007. In a decision issued in 2001, the IACHR reported that members of the New Granada Battalion deprived Leonel de Jesús Isaza Echeverry of his right to life by killing him in 1993. IACHR, *Report N° 64/01, Case 11.712 Colombia: Leonel De Jesús Isaza Echeverry y Otro*. April 6, 2001.

[79] Plutarco Eliécer Molano Jimenez, Prosecutor 28 of Simiti, Cartagena, *Resolution, No 138 050*, May 4, 2007.

[80] Hina Jilani, *Report submitted by the Special Representative of the Secretary-General on the situation of human rights defenders, Addendum – Summary of Cases Transmitted to Governments and Replies Received*, U.N. Doc A/HRC/7/28/Add.1 (March 5, 2008), pp. 115-116.

[81] Constitutional Court, Decision T-444 -92, Judge Alejandro Martinez Caballero.

[82] Constitutional Court Decision T-066 -98, Judge Eduardo Cifuentes Munoz.

[83] Alirio Uribe Munoz, *Defense Brief: Criminal Prosecution Continues against Social Leader of Agrarian Sector, Victor Julio Laguado Boada for the Supposed Crime of Rebellion*, File No. 826036, p. 13, November 2007, citing the *Resolution from the Prosecutor before the National Tribunal*. May 30, 1994.

[84] Rural Association of Rio Cimitarra Valley (ACVC) Case. Prosecutor 37 Human Rights and International Humanitarian Unit of Medellín, *Resolution of Dismissal*, April 23, 2008, p. 18.

[85] *Decision of First Instance*, Pabon, p. 5.

[86] Human Rights First, "Colombian Activists Targeted by Government Assassination Plot," October 5, 2006, available at http://www.humanrightsfirst.org/defenders/hrd_colombia/alert100406_celeyta.htm

[87] Department of Military Intelligence, Colombian Army 3rd Brigade, *Intelligence Report*, May 24, 2003, reference number CIME-RIME3-INT4-252.

[88] Maria Eugenia Lora Castaño, Attorney General's Office, Cali, Letter to Luis Ramirez Rios, CTI, June 23, 2004, reference number FGN CTI SIA 358.

[89] *Judgment*, Superior Criminal Tribunal of Bogotá, No. 158.08, Judge Patricia Rodriguez Torres, September 16, 2008.

[90] Colombian Platform of Democracy, Development and Human Rights, *Undoing the Spell: Alternatives to the Politics of the Government of Álvaro Uribe*, November 2006.

[91] The Prosecutorial Unit for Terrorism in Arauca initiated proceedings against Laguado and subsequently transferred proceedings to Prosecutor 330 of the Bogotá Unit for Offences against Individual Liberty. See Alirio Uribe Muñoz, *Defense Brief: Criminal Prosecution Continues against Social Leader of Agrarian Sector, Victor Julio Laguado Boada for the Supposed Crime of Rebellion*, File No. 826036, pp. 1-2, November 2007.

[92] Ibid., p. 20.

[93] See also U.N. Working Group on Arbitrary Detention, *Opinions Adopted by the Working Group: Opinion No. 30/2006 (Colombia)*, February 2, 2007, A/HRC/4/40/Add.1, p. 112.

[94] Human Rights First, Letter to the Inspector General, September 12, 2008, available at http://www.humanrightsfirst.org/pdf/080915-HRD-letter-colombia-minga.pdf. Intelligence report available at http://www.cipcol.org/files/080917inte.pdf

[95] Juan Carlos Gomez Ramirez, Letter to Human Rights First from Director of Human Rights, Defense Ministry, October 3, 2008.

[96] Ibid.

[97] Criminal Procedural Code, Law 600 of 2000, July 24, 2000, article 234.

[98] Hernando Betancur, *Resolution Resolving Appeal*, Third Prosecutor Medellín, December 6, 2005, p. 5.

[99] *Judgment*, Criminal Court 53, Bogotá Circuit, No. 2006–00366, Judge Carmen Cecilia Arrieta Burgos, June 16, 2008, p. 71.

[100] Judicial inspector 30 of the Public Ministry to the 9th Specialized Prosecution Office, Andres Nanclares Arango, as cited in ibid; Folder 147, File No. 11.

[101] Ibid.

[102] *Judgment*, Criminal Court 53, Bogotá Circuit, No. 2006–00366, Judge Carmen Cecilia Arrieta Burgos, June 16, 2008.

[103] Ibid., p. 74.

[104] See, e.g, Human Rights Watch, *A Wrong Turn: The Record of the Colombian Attorney-General's Office*, Vol. 14(3)(B), 2002.

[105] See, e.g., U.S. State Department, *Country Reports on Human Rights Practices for 2006: Colombia*, Section 1d.

[106] Supreme Court Unit, Prosecutor General's Office, *Resolution Closing Investigation of Amaury Enrique Padilla Cabarcas*, June 3, 2004, File No. 8278, p. 40.

[107] Human Rights First interview with Danilo Rueda, Director, Inter-Church Commission for Justice and Peace, November 20, 2008.

[108] Coordination Colombia, Europe and United States (CCEEUU), *Liberty: Hostage to Democratic Security*, April 6, 2006.

[109] Ibid.

[110] Córdoba was in the Interior and Justice Ministry's protection program for at-risk social leaders due to threats against her life. See also Inter-American Commission on Human Rights, *Precautionary Measures 2002: Precautionary Measures Granted or Extended by the Commission*, April 19, 2002, available at http://www.iachr.org/medidas/2002.eng.htm

[111] Coordination Colombia, Europe and United States (CCEEUU), *Liberty: Hostage to Democratic Security*, April 6, 2006.

[112] Ibid.

[113] First Criminal Court of the Arauca Specialized Circuit in Clearing Backlogs.

[114] In October 2002, the IACHR granted Cedeño precautionary measures after death threats from high-level paramilitary commanders: Inter-American Commission on Human Rights, *Precautionary Measures 2002*.

[115] Alirio Uribe Muñoz, *Defense Brief: Criminal Prosecution Continues against Lawyer Teresa de Jesus Cedeño and Another for the Supposed Crime of Bribery*, Bogota, August 15, 2007, p. 1.

[116] Decision of Second Instance, *Resolving Appeal to Resolution of Accusation*, November 4, 2005, cited in ibid., p. 40.

[117] Prosecutor 37, Human Rights and International Humanitarian Unit of Medellín, *Resolution of Dismissal*, April 23, 2008, p. 16.

[118] See also case of Diego Figeuoroa, who was reportedly detained without an arrest warrant in November 2005 and was allegedly abused by the police and denied access to his lawyer. In dismissing the charges a prosecutor stated, "He has been obliged to live in places where daily existence exposes people to all kinds of risks, given the scarce presence of the state, so that when they are visited by [subversive groups] they should attend to them, greet them, share brief moments with them in order to avoid abuses or executions as from time to time have occurred... these interactions alone cannot be said to show that Diego Figueroa is a member of a subversive group and he has not therefore committed the presumed crime." Prosecutor 38, Criminal Court Circuit Buenaventura, *Resolution of Dismissal*, June 20, 2006, p. 3.

[119] Article 322, Law 600 of 2000, Criminal Procedural Code, July 24, 2000.

[120] From February 11, 2004 to March 7, 2005. See Lucia Giraldo Prosecutor 153, Unit for Offences against the Constitutional Regime, *Resolution of Dismissal*, September 19, 2005, p 16.

[121] MINGA, *Defense Brief: The Unjust Persecution and Criminalization of Human Rights and Violation of Procedural Fairness*, p 4, 2004.

[122] ACVC, *Andrés Gil, Political Prisoner, Unable to Attend International Forum on Human Rights* ,November 20, 2007, p 5, available at http://www.prensarural.org/spip/spip.php?article871

[123] Article 29 of the Colombian Constitution states: "Every person is presumed innocent until they have been declared judicially guilty. Defendants have the right to the defense and assistance of a lawyer of their choosing, during the investigation and the prosecution; to due process without unwarranted delays; to present evidence and to dispute evidence that has been gathered against them.... Any evidence obtained in violation of due process is null and void." See also articles 126, 176 and 323 Criminal Procedural Code and Constitutional Court Decision C-096-03, Judge Manuel José Cepeda Espinosa, February 11, 2003.

[124] Decisión C-096-03, Judge Manuel José Cepeda Espinosa, February 11, 2003.

[125] MINGA, *Defense Brief: The Unjust Persecution and Criminalization of Human Rights and Violation of Procedural Fairness*, 2004.

[126] Oral hearing, no sentencing documents available. See Inter-Church Justice and Peace Commission, *Militares Anuncian Operaciones Paramilitares Contra La Población, Persisten Hostigamientos Contra Aldemar Lozano y Familia*, April 8, 2008, p. 2. See also Human Rights First, "Stop Arbitrary Detention of Colombian Activists," January 31, 2008, available at http://www.humanrightsfirst.org/defenders/hrd_colombia/alert013108_TorresH.htm; Inter-Church Justice and Peace Commission, *Report 53, Meta Puerto Esperanza.Arbitrary Detention Aldemar Lozano*, December 25, 2007, p.1

[127] United Nations, Working Group on Arbitrary Detention, *Revised Methods of Work*, December 19, 1997, rule 8(a) U.N. Doc E/CN.4/1998/44 Annex 1.

[128] Colombian Platform of Democracy, Development and Human Rights, *Undoing the Spell: Alternatives to the Politics of the Government of Álvaro Uribe*, November 2006, p. 168.

[129] Human Rights First interview with members of Colombian civil society, Bogotá, November 7, 2007.

[130] See generally Colombian Platform of Democracy, Development and Human Rights, *Undoing the Spell: Alternatives to the Politics of the Government of Álvaro Uribe*, November 2006, p. 170.

[131] Criminal Procedural Code, Law 600 of 2000, Official Diary No.44.097, July 24, 2000, article 350.

[132] Human Rights First, Letter to Prosecutor-General, November 5, 2008, available at http://www.humanrightsfirst.org/pdf/HRD-081110-sandoval-detention-no-sig.pdf

[133] Reiniciar, "We Deplore the Detention of 13 Social Leaders in Arauca," press release, November 4, 2008.

[134] See e.g. Hernan Durango, "Human Rights Commission Denounces Grave Humanitarian Situation in Arauca," *Colombia Indymedia*, February 2, 2008, available at http://colombia.indymedia.org/news/2008/02/79200.php

[135] Criminal Procedural Code, Articles 3 and 356. See also Constitutional Court jurisprudence: e.g. Decision C-77401, Judge Rodrigo Escobar Gil, July 25, 2001.

[136] Ibid.

[137] Tito Augusto Gaitan, *Defense Brief to Maria Cristina Ramirez, Judges of Saravena Criminal Circuit: Support of the Appeal of the Unjust Decision of against Araucan Human Rights Defenders and Social Leaders,* File No. 2004-298. p 9.

[138] Third Prosecutor before the Barrancabermeja Criminal Circuit, *Resolution of Dismissal*, October 29, 2007, p. 3.

[139] Ibid., p 4.

[140] Ibid.

[141] See e.g. the following cases in the Annex: Diego Figueroa, Teofilo Acuna, Juan Carlos Celis Gonzalez.

[142] See e.g. the following cases in the Annex: Juan Carlos Celis Gonzalez, Claudia Montoya, Arauca defenders/José Murillo Tobo.

[143] See e.g. the following cases in the Annex: Teresa de Jesús Cedeño Galíndez, Luz Perly Cordoba Mosquera, Diego Figueroa.

[144] Colombian Criminal Code, Law 599 of 2000, Official Diary No 44.097, July 24, 2000.

[145] Hina Jilani, *Annual Report by Special Representative of the Secretary-General on Human Rights Defenders*, U.N. Doc. E/CN.4/2005/101, para. 54, March 16, 2005.

[146] Organization of American States, Inter-American Commission on Human Rights, *Report on the Situation of Human Rights Defenders in the Americas.* OEA/Ser.L/V/II.124 Doc. 5 rev.1, March 7, 2006, para 81.

[147] The case is being investigated by Prosecution Office 64 in Bogotá. Memo provided to Human Rights First by Reinaldo Villalba (Duque's lawyer), July 28, 2008.

[148] Reporters Without Borders, "Government Tries to Suspend Security Measures for Journalist Despite Recent Murder Contract and Paramilitary Threats," Press Release, October 31, 2007, available at http://www.protectionline.org/Claudia-Julieta-Duque-Government.html

[149] Investigation Number 70763.

[150] Human Rights First, "Colombian Human Rights Leader Iván Cepeda Receives the 2007 Roger Baldwin Award," press release, June 2007, available at http://www.humanrightsfirst.org/defenders/baldwin/2007/

[151] Corporación Colectivo de Abogados José Alvear Restrepo, *Señalamientos y Hostigamientos contra Iván Cepeda Castro*, DR-002/07, May 14, 2007.

[152] Iván Cepeda, Speech Delivered to Citizen Hearing, San Onofre, Sucre, November 28, 2006, p. 4, available in Spanish at: http://www.movimientodevictimas.org/node/254; Translated excerpts of Cepeda's statement are in Center for International Policy, "The Victims' Movement and the View from San Onofre," Sucre, December 7, 2006, available at http://www.cipcol.org/?p=311

[153] Ibid.

[154] United Nations, Working Group on Arbitrary Detention, *Opinions Adopted by the Working Group on Arbitrary Detention: Opinion No. 30/2006 (Colombia)*, February 2, 2007, U.N. Doc: A/HRC/4/40/Add.1 p. 113.

[155] Luis Camilo Osorio Isaza, Prosecutor-General, *Resolution No 0-1678*, May 3, 2005.

[156] See United Nations, *Declaration on the Right and Responsibility of Individuals, Groups and Organs of Society to Promote and Protect Universally Recognized Human Rights and Fundamental Freedoms*, A/RES/53/144, March 8, 1999.

[157] *The Department of State, Foreign Operations and Related Programs Appropriations Act, 2008 (Consolidated Appropriations Act, 2008)* HR 2764, Public Law No: 110-161, December 26, 2007.

[158] Colombian Inspector General, *Conclusions of the Working Group Inspector General – Minster of Defense Regarding Criteria to Revise Military Intelligence Reports*, No 285, March 15, 2007.

[159] See Inspector General, Point 19: Advances, *Difficulties and Challenges in 2007 in the Revision of the Applicable Criteria and Information to be Included in Intelligence Reports*, November 2007.

[160] Ibid.

[161] Ibid. See also Colonel Juan Carlos Gomez Ramirez, Letter to Human Rights First from Director of Human Rights, National Defense Ministry, File No. 76792/MDD-HH-725, October 3, 2008.

[162] Colombian Congress, *Bill on Intelligence and Counter-Intelligence* (178/07; 180/07; 183/07 and 211/01 Accumulated; Approved for second time by the Senate on June 3, 2008 and subsequently approved for a third time).

[163] For more details see Human Rights First, Letter to Colombian Congress re: Intelligence Bill, June 10, 2008, available at http://www.humanrightsfirst.info/pdf/080612-HRD-colombia-sen-intel.pdf

[164] *See also*, Office of the United Nations High Commissioner for Human Rights in Colombia, *Annual Report 2005* (Commission on Human Rights, Sixty-second session), May 16, 2006, E/CN.4/2006/9, p. 32.

[165] Article 15 of the Colombian Constitution states, "All people . . . have the right to know, access and rectify information that has been collected about them in date bases and archives of public and private entities."

[166] Prosecutor Rodrigo Rodriguez Barragan, Prosecutor Unit 26 Bucaramanga. *Resolution of Preclusion of Investigation*, June 3, 2003, p.10.

[167] Lucia Giraldo Prosecutor 153, Unit for Offenses against the Constitutional Regime, *Resolution of Dismissal*, September 19, 2005, p. 12.

[168] See, e.g., President of the Republic, *Presidential Directive 7 of 1999: Support, Exchange and Collaboration of the State with Human Rights Organizations*, September 9, 1999.

[169] See e.g., Inter-American Court of Human Rights, *Kimel v Argentina*, May 2, 2008, available at http://www.corteidh.or.cr/docs/casos/articulos/seriec_177_esp.doc ; Inter-American Court of Human Rights, Herrera Ulloa v Costa Rica, July 2, 2004, available at http://www.corteidh.or.cr/docs/casos/articulos/seriec_107_ing.doc ; Special Rapporteur for Freedom of Expression, *Annual Report Of 2002*, Chapter V, which states, "In order to ensure that freedom of expression is properly defended, states should reform their criminal libel, slander and defamation laws so that only civil penalties may be applied in the case of offenses against public officials. In addition, liability for offenses against public officials should only occur in cases of 'actual malice.' 'Actual malice' means that the author of the statement in question acted with the intention to cause harm was aware that the statement was false or acted with reckless disregard for the truth or falsity of the statement."

[170] Inter-American Court of Human Rights, *Kimel v Argentina*, May 2, 2008, available at http://www.corteidh.or.cr/docs/casos/articulos/seriec_177_esp.doc

[171] Inter-American Commission on Human Rights, *1994 Annual Report, Chapter V Report on the Compatibility of "Desacato" Laws with the American Convention on Human Rights*, February 17, 1995, OEA/Ser. L/V/II.88, doc. 9 rev. pp. 197-212, available at http://www.cidh.org/annualrep/94eng/chap.5.htm

[172] In April 2007, Mexico decriminalized libel and slander. El Salvador has also removed these offenses from their criminal law, available at http://www.ifex.org/en/content/view/full/82567.

www.ingramcontent.com/pod-product-compliance
Lightning Source LLC
Chambersburg PA
CBHW081723270326
41933CB00017B/3274